WORKPLACE SECRETS REVEALED

PASSING THE BATON TO THE NEXT GENERATION

ALAN L. OPPENHEIMER

Editing by The Pro Book Editor
Interior and Cover Design by IAPS.rocks

ISBN: 978-1-7350860-1-9

    1. Main category—SELF-HELP
    2. Other category—EDUCATION

First Edition

This book is dedicated to Linda Morrissey, Richard Falk, Ellen Solov, Sally Fallis, Jeanie Pemberton, Diane Williams and Julie Rehder, who helped me through a difficult time in my life.

TABLE OF CONTENTS

INTRODUCTION

AFTER TWELVE, SIXTEEN, OR EVEN more years focused on your education and expending precious resources—time, sweat, equity, and money—now you're ready to start your career. Welcome to a new world that will not always make sense. More often than not, the transition from working on an education to working toward building a career can be quite surprising and unsettling. Much of what you learned in school may not apply in this new environment of policy, procedures, office politics, corporate speak, goals and objectives, and company vision.

This book provides insight and direction for dealing with many issues and conundrums you will encounter in the workplace. Why stumble through the discovery process of how things work when you can get a head start on the learning curve that exists any time we embark on new endeavors?

The many voices of experience presented in this book

are meant to inspire discussions about your career path, to help you with planning ahead, and teach you about important touchstones that will influence your success.

Most people with forty years of work experience behind them did not understand the environment they were entering after their formal education ended. This book is the "easy button" so you can benefit from the experiences of a variety of experienced managers and executives without having to attend the same school of hard knocks.

I hope you find useful and thought-provoking information that resonates with you and helps smooth your road. Best wishes to you for much success and happiness over the years to come!

YOUR CHALLENGES VERSUS THOSE OF OTHER GENERATIONS

YOU MAY THINK THAT YOUR challenges are greater than those of generations before you. Am I right? It's natural—every generation feels this way until they gain enough life/work experience to broaden their viewpoint.

We all remember hearing how hard previous generations had it. My parents told me they walked miles to school, uphill both ways and in the snow. Everyone has heard some variation of this. It's how our parents attempt to help us see that life struggles are not a new concept and that we will be okay. They made it, so you will too.

Growing up in the 1950s and '60s, many baby boomers did not have the following things:

-Color TVs

-Cable, or often, more than one TV channel

- Air-conditioned homes and cars

- Calculators

- Cell phones

- Computers

- Internet

- Alexa

- Anything remotely like there is today for listening to music

What we did have:

- Rotary dial phones

- Drive-in movie theaters

- Car radios were AM only, then AM/FM, then eight-track, then cassette, then CDs, and now streaming, Blue Tooth, and satellite

- Huge and expensive multi-volume encyclopedia sets

- Stagflation during President Jimmy Carter's administration in the late-1970s, where price inflation was out of control, wages did not keep up, jobs were hard to find, and there were long lines at the gas pump and gas shortages

- The Great Recession in 2008 and 2009, and the prospect of another recession headed our way, courtesy of COVID-19

- Heroin and crack drug abuse, now replaced by opioid and fentanyl addictions

-Richard Nixon, George Wallace, and Lester Maddox. You have Donald Trump and Nancy Pelosi

-The Vietnam War draft

-Hitler, communism, nuclear war, and AIDS. You have the stigma that previous generations put on the "entitlement" generations, and certainly the most defining event in your life—COVID-19—and associated recession and competition for well-paying jobs.

Safety

The US is safer today than it was in the late '60s, but the media does not want you to believe that because good news doesn't help ratings. But burglaries and murders are down. You would not know that by listening to politicians or companies selling protective equipment. Terrorism and hate crimes are the larger concern for today's generation. Deaths from car accidents are down dramatically in spite of texting while driving because roads and cars are safer.

Medical

People are living longer today, partly due to the decline in smoking and improved health care. In the '60s, medical specialties were a rare breed. Most medical services were provided by general practitioners and consisted of an X-ray and a shot of penicillin. Today, we have a multitude of specialists and a vast array of new medicines, which helps explain why our health care costs are so high. Another reason for higher medical costs is that we are living longer, and the aging population requires more medical care. Improvement in medicine has increased the cure rate for many dreaded diseases, and vaccines have eliminated some contagious illnesses, but not all and not yet. Today, we are dealing with COVID-19, but for the most part, we do not have malaria, polio, measles, mumps, etc.

Social Justice

For the most part, we are more tolerant and accepting as a nation to LBGTQ, gender equality, and race-relation issues. More tolerance and improvement is needed in the world to be fair and equal, but we have made huge strides. Until the late '60s, some states prohibited marriage between people of different races. Until the '70s, homosexuality was considered a mental disorder by the psychiatric profession. And there are many more examples of bias and racism that have changed drastically over the last several decades.

Environment

Prior to the early '70s, nuclear waste was dumped into the ocean, and holes in the ozone that protect us from solar radiation were discovered. Since the early '70s, emissions have dropped significantly, many polluted dumps have been cleaned, and ocean dumping of nuclear waste has been banned. Cars and manufacturing plants are more efficient and cleaner. In addition, technologies continue to develop in a variety of areas, including electric cars, solar panels, wind power, etc. to improve the environment.

Challenges remain for the next generation(s), such as global warming, plastics in our oceans and in our landfills, and so on. I remember visiting Pompeii, an advanced civilization destroyed by volcanic lava from Mt. Vesuvius in 79 A.D. About three-fourths of the city has been excavated, the remaining parts left undisturbed for future generations to explore. Similarly, previous generations have dealt with and solved numerous problems in things such as medicine, domestic and international security, human rights, the environment, and technology, but problems remain for future generations to solve.

Previous generations made progress but did not finish the tasks of solving all of the world's problems. We may have failed in the execution, but we did not fail in ambition. You have every right to be scared by the enormity of the tasks before you, but I know that you will rise to the occasion to make the world a better place for yourself, your children, and future generations.

You certainly have challenges, and big ones, but so did all the generations before you. We made it, and you will too. You are not alone as you launch into self-supporting adulthood. As many of us retirees look back at our lives, the following proverb resonates. If you think about this proverb while you are young, you may benefit from its wisdom,

"Too soon we're old. Too late we're smart."

—Old proverb, source unknown

What can you do about getting old too soon? Other than use the time you have wisely, probably nothing. Don't postpone those things you can do now until later. As you get older, you don't have the vigor, physical fitness, and desire of a young person. So if you want to travel or start a physical activity like sailing or board surfing, do it sooner rather than later. Develop and gather interests and hobbies while you are young. Your old self will be most appreciative.

What can you do about getting smart too late? Recognize that you don't know what you don't know and avail yourself of every opportunity to learn. Read, take classes, and listen to people who are well-informed or have specific knowledge. Young people tend to overestimate their knowledge of the world and how it works—or how it should work—and underestimate the value of seeking wisdom from generations before them. In reality, we gain smartness and understanding over years of experience. If this is true, and I believe it to be so, we should take every advantage to gain knowledge sooner rather than later, and that is the impetus of this book.

Some quotes from the unknown to some of the most successful people in their field may also be helpful.

"You will never feel 100 percent ready when an opportunity arises. So just do it."

—Unknown

"One of the greatest gifts you can give yourself, right here, right now, in this single, solitary, monumental moment in your life, is to decide, without apology, to commit to the journey, and not to the outcome."

—Joyce DiDonato, opera singer
(Juilliard School Commencement Speech, 2014)

"But my fear of failure never approached in magnitude my fear of what if. ... For many of you who maybe don't have it all figured out, it's okay. ... Enjoy the process of your search without succumbing to the pressure of the result. Trust your gut, keep throwing darts at the dartboard. Don't listen to the critics and you will figure it out."

—Will Ferrell, comedian
(USC Commencement Speech, 2017)

"I think a lot of people dream. And while they are busy dreaming, the really happy people, the really successful people, the really interesting, engaged, powerful people, are busy doing."

—Shonda Rhimes, television producer, television and film writer, and author
(Dartmouth College Commencement Speech, 2014)

"You cannot dream of becoming something you do not know about. You have to learn to dream big. Education exposes you to what the world has to offer…"

—Supreme Court Justice Sonia Sotomayor
(Commencement speech at Manhattan
College, New York City, 17 May 2019).

"How can we stop the evil in the future if we pretend it never happened in the past?"

—Unknown

SHOULD YOU GO TO COLLEGE?

OLLEGE AND/OR GRADUATE SCHOOL IS a wonderful thing for many people, as it prepares you for careers that require a college education and/or a graduate degree. But is college right for you? Some students attend college but never graduate, or they take courses that have little marketable significance, and worst of all, they accumulate significant debt that hangs over their heads for years.

A good place to start answering the question would be talking with your high school guidance counselor. Talk about what you want to do and what you do not want to do. If this discussion points to college, carefully look at the cost and anticipated debt at graduation. For the 2018-2019 academic year, the average tuition and fees was $8,000 for in-state students and $22,000 for out-of-state students. Private schools are substantially more expensive. Add another $10,000 to $13,000 for room and board. If you live at home and attend an in-state school, your cost would be at the low end of $8,000 per year—or

$32,000 for a four-year degree. If you attend an out-of-state school, you are looking at $32,000 to $35,000 per year—or $128,000 to $140,000 for a four-year degree.

If you finance your degree, it might take a long time—maybe decades—to pay off, especially if you land a low-level salaried or hourly job. Compare your anticipated salary to your total debt and look at the years it will take to pay off, but don't forget to consider your living expenses too. What is left over after your living expenses is all you will have each month to pay against your college debt, though the lender will treat your loan like any other lender does and expect consistent payments that take priority in your budget. And be aware that current bankruptcy law does not relieve student loan debt.

If your ideal career path won't support the cost of a college education, consider the alternative. There are many jobs that do not require a college degree. There is a significant mismatch of available vocational and technical jobs versus available workforce, so employers are having a difficult time finding skilled workers in the areas of manufacturing, transportation, construction, auto mechanics for high-end cars, and production of machines or tools. And many of these job opportunities pay more than college graduate jobs, some paying six-figure wages.[1]

If you don't get educated, you are screwed, but this does not mean you need a four-year college degree. We currently have a national crisis of college graduates who are

---

1   Schnurman, Mitchell. March 2020. "Collin College's new tech school saves time and money, and promises high-paying jobs." *Dallas Morning News.* https://www.dallasnews.com/business/jobs/2020/03/10/collin-colleges-new-tech-school-saves-time-and-money-and-promises-high-paying-jobs/

underemployed and cannot pay their college debt. You may be much better off with a marketable, vocational, or technical skill and without a large debt clouding your future. By planning ahead and leveraging all the tools and resources available, you can focus your education expenses on training in a specific skill of interest. That also makes sense when you consider long-term cost and return on investment.

Simply searching the Internet will reveal a lot of information about jobs in demand that do not require a four-year degree. Some will require vocational or technical training, and some may require a two-year Associates Degree. Here are a few examples:

> https://www.trade-schools.net/articles/best-jobs-for-introverts

> https://www.thebalancecareers.com/best-trade-school-graduate-jobs-4125189

> https://www.indeed.com/career-advice/finding-a-job/highest-paying-trade-jobs

If you choose to go to college, there are many universities and colleges with wonderful regional reputations and a few with national and worldwide reputations, such as Harvard, Princeton, Yale, Brown, Cornell, Dartmouth, University of Pennsylvania, Georgetown, University of California Berkley, Wharton, and so on. Attending a school with a national or worldwide reputation has many advantages. If you are accepted and can arrange tuition, you should go.

With regionally well-known schools, the benefits of their reputation are regional, so it is of little benefit to attend an expensive school with a regional reputation in the northeast if you do not plan to live in the northeast. Unless you go to one of the top fifty schools in the nation, it doesn't make a whole lot of difference on your resume. One of the most important overlooked factors in school selection is the quality of the career-services department helping you get a job. As you can see, it's very important to make sure the investment you make in your education is the right fit for your long-term goals and ability to pay off that debt.

Nobody talks about forgiving trade-school debt because trade-school graduates can pay their own way. From the National Center for Construction Education & Research survey shown in the Dallas Morning News, the following list shows average annual salaries in 2018, not including overtime, per diem, or other incentives for a few trades that do not require a four-year degree:

Project Supervisor	$ 88,365
Combo Welder	$ 71,067
Instrumentation Tech	$ 70,080
Mobile Crane Operator	$ 66,119
HVAC Tech	$ 62,472
Commercial Electrician	$ 61,139
Plumber	$ 59,627
Commercial Carpenter	$ 56,877
Mason	$ 56,784

In the construction industry, just one out of ten workers is female. This represents an opportunity for women since some construction companies are aggressively recruiting and promoting women. This change in workplace culture is due partly to addressing a deepening labor shortage, partly to bring more diversity to corporate thinking and client interactions, and partly because women are so badly underrepresented. [2]

Women may be reluctant to enter construction because they're concerned about lifting building materials and handling heavy equipment. Others may be put off by the prospect of working in a male-dominated field. But unlike in past decades, there are government rules and corporate policies to protect women, and good companies make sure female employees have a mentor to help navigate an unconventional workplace. Most women in the construction industry don't work on job sites. They're much more likely to be in an office setting, handling project estimates, design, human resources, and the like. They may not be building on-site, but they are building virtually.

According to an article in the *Dallas Morning News* written by Mitchel Schnurman,[3] Collin College Technical Campus—just north of Dallas, TX—offers training, certificates, and associate degrees in many specialized career paths, including carpentry, plumbing, automo-

2   Schnurman, Mitchell. March 2020. "Help wanted: Why the construction industry is recruiting more women." *Dallas Morning News.* https://www.dallasnews.com/business/jobs/2020/03/06/help-wanted-why-the-construction-industry-is-recruiting-more-women/
3   Schnurman, Mitchell. March 2020. "Collin College's new tech school saves time and money, and promises high-paying jobs." *Dallas Morning News.* https://www.dallasnews.com/business/jobs/2020/03/10/collin-colleges-new-tech-school-saves-time-and-money-and-promises-high-paying-jobs/

tive, electronics, welding, and a range of health sciences. These so-called middle skills are in high demand and pay middle-class wages with the potential to reach six figures. Not only can earnings from these jobs actually rival—and sometimes exceed—the average pay for positions requiring a bachelor's degree, but these paths require just two years of post-secondary training and no student debt that follows one into the workplace.

Schnurman went on to write:

> The payoff? According to data compiled by Collin College, several jobs paid over $50,000 in average salaries in 2018. Construction managers earned six figures, and computer network support specialists were paid $80,000, the school said.

> A recent report from Georgetown University examined "the overlooked value of certificates and associate's degrees." About 2 million such credentials are awarded annually in the US, on par with the total number of bachelor's degrees.

> Depending on the specialty, some workers can earn more than those with a bachelor's degree, netting a higher return on their time, effort, and money.

> "As a result, less education can often be worth more," the report said.

> Other parts of the country are coming to the same conclusion as Collin College: That the middle-

skills job sector is robust and growing and offers a solid pathway to the middle class, said Anthony Carnevale, co-author of the Georgetown report.

"There's a message, especially to young people, that this is cool and necessary," said Carnevale, director of Georgetown's Center on Education and the Workforce. "And the community is willing to spend real money on it and give you first-class treatment."

Employers repeatedly told school leaders they wanted graduates to also have soft skills, especially in verbal and written communication. Collin College's associate degree includes fifteen hours of core classes in humanities, English, communication and the like.

That sequence is also helpful if workers decide to eventually get a bachelor's or master's, which is a popular route for those pursuing jobs in management.[4]

There are significantly different college and career path options in demand and available today, so while this chapter does not seek to discourage anyone from getting a higher education, it does intend to broaden the reader's perspective so they can choose wisely.

---

4   Schnurman, Mitchell. March 2020. "Collin College's new tech school saves time and money, and promises high-paying jobs." *Dallas Morning News.* https://www.dallasnews. com/business/jobs/2020/03/10/collin-colleges-new-tech-school-saves-time-and-money-and-promises-high-paying-jobs/

DO YOU NEED A MENTOR?

I F YOU ARE READING THIS, I am guessing that you are young, smart, and aggressive. As you prepare to enter the workforce, it's important to understand there is still a lot to learn that the classroom environment cannot teach. It doesn't matter what career path you choose—business, medical, legal, the arts, technical skills, etc.—learning and doing are two very different experiences.

You wouldn't play football or any other organized sport without a coach, or take up skiing or golf without lessons, so why take chances with your career?

You're about to engage in a new game that will span forty-plus years. This new game will be on a different playing field, with different rules, and there will be multiple answers or approaches to countless situations. You will need a strategy to leverage your hard-earned education and propel your new career forward so you can get the most out of all that you've invested in yourself so far. So how does a new hire make the right plays in this strange new arena?

Some would say work hard, keep your head down and your nose clean, and you will move up the ranks. Maybe, but why not optimize your chances of success by having a mentor who can share his/her perspective on scenarios you will certainly encounter for the first time, but the same scenarios that have played out in every organization from the beginning of time?

Examples:

- What if you have the boss from hell or the subordinate from hell?

- What if you planned a three-day weekend vacation, and the boss asks you to work the weekend to make a deadline?

- How do you handle a new subordinate that has twenty years of experience compared to your six months of experience?

- Why did you not get the promotion, and how do you get promoted next time? What are you doing that you should not, and what are you not doing that you should?

- How do you motivate your team?

- How do you handle ethical issues, like being asked to post an accounting entry that isn't completely accurate, and your boss justifies the entry as "for the good of the team?"

- Strategic issues: If you are an entrepreneur and

start your own business or are involved with your family's business, ways you can grow the company:

- Should you hire from within or through recruiting?

- How do you finance the growth?

- How much debt is too much?

- When putting the annual budget together, should it be realistic or aggressive, and what are the tradeoffs?

- How do you handle unreasonable customers?

- How do you deal with coworkers who don't follow the rules, create more work and/or unhappy customers you'll have to take care of?

That is but a small sampling of issues where gaining perspective and direction from a mentor can help you maximize a positive outcome. There are no easy answers, and any answer will require more information and discussion. Having someone you can go to who has lived and breathed these issues far longer than you only makes sense.

As a young man, I did not feel the need for a mentor. I felt that I knew it all or would figure it out. I also felt that my father's experiences had come from the dark ages and were no longer relevant—what a mistake. I didn't know what I didn't know.

My father was the VP of Operations for a manufacturing plant. I became a CPA in public accounting, later in corporate accounting and finance. Although our career paths were very different, there were many overlapping areas, such as working with superiors, peers, subordinates, and the corporate entity. My father would have been a wonderful mentor, as he had been to others, but I wouldn't hear or accept his advice. I was clueless in a world that was unfamiliar to me but certain that I knew it all and could change the world on my own. By the time I figured out the error in my ways, too much valuable time had passed, and too many mistakes in judgment had been made. In hindsight, my father would have been the best possible mentor for me. He had my best interests at heart and the time and willingness to mentor me. So if this situation sounds familiar, put your pride aside and don't be too headstrong to listen to a parent's advice.

If not your parent, how do you choose the right mentor?

Here is one of the best mentoring stories I've ever heard.

Carl Sewell's father owned an automobile dealership in Dallas. Carl looked forward to learning the business and taking it over one day, but he felt the need for a mentor—someone outside of the family. After many months of phone calls and letters, Stanley Marcus—the co-founder of Neiman Marcus—agreed to meet Carl for lunch. After their first lunch, they met for lunch once a month for the next fifteen years. Carl now owns one of the most respected car dealers in the country, is the author of *Customers for Life*, and is on target to own and operate fifty auto dealerships across the nation.

Carl mentions Stanley Marcus on numerous occasions in

his book and in a speech to an executive group, where he tells the story of how Stanley Marcus became his mentor. He said that Mr. Marcus was instrumental to his success in providing excellent customer service and growing his business. Probably the most important takeaway was that quality and value always win.

You may ask why Carl chose and sought out Stanley Marcus in the first place. I believe he sensed there was a link between fine clothing and cars when it came to delivering exceptional customer service. Perhaps he realized that cars—especially luxury cars—were not a commodity, and he wanted to better understand his target market's needs and how to give them exceptional customer service.

Carl struck gold with his mentor, but what did Stanley Marcus get out of the deal, and why did he agree to meet with Carl over a fifteen-year period? Experienced executives in the twilight of their career love to tell stories and welcome an eager audience. They like to give advice, and even more, they like to hear how their advice works out. Having a mentor is a two-way deal, like any other relationship. You have to give to receive. That is, Carl did not provide an endless list of problems for Stanley to solve. Much of the time, he listened to Stanley's stories and worked out how to apply the life lessons to his specific situation.

If you are still in high school or college but have not decided what you want to do for a living, start laying the groundwork for building professional relationships by talking to people already in the workforce about what they do for a living. If you have already graduated and started work, start with the relationships already developed and add new relationships. Maybe these conversations will align with your interests as sources of information to help you select your field of study and/or to map out your career-pathing goals. You might have family, friends, or friends of classmates that would be good candidates. Go talk to them. Ask them what they do. If they give you a short one-liner, ask them to elaborate. Ask how they decided on their career. Engage them with open-ended questions and let them talk without interruption. If they ask why you want to know, tell them you are trying to figure out what you want to study and what kind of professional career you want. The goal is not to have a mentor at the end of the conversation, but to begin a relationship for future questions and discussions. And as Carl's example shows, choose voices of experience.

After talking to several people, you will be in a position to identify a mentor target that is compatible with you. There are no hard-and-fast rules for mentors, and it doesn't have to be a pairing that lasts for the life of your career. Instead, it may be more appropriate to occasionally make a call to one of your many contacts to discuss an issue you are having at work. After your contact spends that time sharing experiences with you, be sure to follow up with them and share your progress.

If you find one or two people you believe will be good mentor material, *do not* ask them to be your mentor right away, as this is a major commitment, and you do not want to pop the question until the time is right. Timing is everything, and you will know when the time is right. Continue developing the relationship by periodically contacting them to discuss various issues, always being respectful and always asking if they have time to talk. You need to do most of the listening and be sure not to overstay your welcome. If the time spent with your potential mentor(s) is useful and win-win for all parties, the right time to commit to a mentoring relationship will present itself naturally.

You most likely will not find someone with Stanley Marcus's stature to be your mentor. Carl was able to land Stanley Marcus as a mentor because his family was in the same social circles as Mr. Marcus. Your family's circle of friends may not be in the top social circle, but it is probably larger than you realize, especially if you consider friends of friends. Also, having "achieved high levels of success" is not a must-have for selecting a mentor. Relevant experience is more important, though a high level of success is nice to have. A successful person is not necessarily a good mentor. It only means they have mastered a discipline and monetized it.

Your company's code of conduct can serve as a model for the ideal mentor, and having a positive attitude will enhance your self-confidence for approaching potential mentors. These things will put you head and shoulders above the competition.

If you work for a large organization, you may find someone in the organization who could be an exceptional mentor. There are business coaches and life coaches who "mentor" for a fee, though I do not recommend this for people new to the workplace, as there should be people in your network who have experienced what you are going through and are—most likely—willing to help you just from a "pay it forward" perspective. I do recommend paid consultants for seasoned executives struggling with a specific issue.

Preferably, there needs to be a link between your career goals and your mentor's experience. Although Carl Sewell was not in the luxury clothing business like Stanley Marcus, they both were in the business of providing the very best customer service for luxury products. Additionally, along the way, Carl Sewell picked up other mentors and/or consultants to help streamline processes necessary to improve both efficiency and customer service.

A mentor should be a been-there-done-that person who has at least one responsibility similar to your responsibilities. There might be a one-for-one relationship, like having the same position, or one or two areas of your responsibilities are the same, like managing shipping operations and supervision of frontline staff. A one-size-fits-all mentor is generally a leader who is successful in a changing environment. This would include turning a failing business into a profitable business or successfully navigating organizational change such as mergers and acquisitions, reorganizations, or systems changes. This type of mentor has a broad understanding of what makes people successful. Look for that person.

Your mentor will be an important part of your network, and through them, you have the opportunity to meet other successful people. Leverage the opportunities—successful people hang together.

Finding a mentor is not necessarily a one-and-done proposition. As you grow in your position and your responsibilities and needs change, your mentor(s) may need to change as well.

Regardless of whether you graduated from high school, trade school, or college, a mentor can be a huge benefit. And don't forget to pay it forward. Even though you need a mentor, there are others who can use your wisdom to help move forward in life, especially children. Paying it forward will also help hone your skillset in your journey to finding your best mentor.

Whether or not you find a mentor, always mirror the actions of successful people. Learn from the individuals in your organization who have a positive and upward trajectory as well as from other successful people you meet along the way. Choose your friends carefully and spend time with people who have positive goals and aspirations you can learn from.

A special thanks to Carl Sewell for sharing his story.

MATCHING PERSONALITY TRAITS AND TALENTS TO CAREER

MATCHING YOUR PERSONALITY TRAITS TO the traits most commonly found in your career choice is an important exercise to help ensure success and comfort in your vocation. One of the most popular and respected aptitude tests available is the Myers-Briggs Type Indicator (MBTI)[5], which is an introspective self-report questionnaire that indicates differing psychological preferences in how people make decisions and perceive the world. It is based on the belief that people experience the world using four principal psychological functions—sensation, intuition, feeling, and thinking—and that one of these four functions will be dominant most of the time. Identifying your natural tendencies will help you identify the right career path, and it will position you to enjoy your work and achieve the levels of success you desire.

5   https://www.mbtionline.com/

The Myers-Briggs Type Indicator (MBTI) aptitude test identifies your four personality traits out of eight. You are either:

- **Extrovert (E) or Introvert (I)**

  - Do you prefer to have a lot of social interaction and gain energy from staying busy and being in the company of many others? Or do you prefer to spend time alone or with just a small number of close friends or loved ones?

- **Sensing (S) or Intuition (N)**

  - Do you most trust in what you can see, smell, hear, taste, or touch in the present moment (i.e., facts), or do you use your intuition and trust your hunches first?

- **Thinking (T) or Feeling (F)**

  - Do you place a high value on logic and con-sistent reasoning when making decisions? Or do you rely on feeling to consider the needs of everyone involved in a particular decision or situation?

- **Judging (J) or Perceiving (P)**

  - Do you prefer a lifestyle that looks fairly struc-tured and routine? Are you orderly, disciplined, and less open to new information? Or do you have a preference for being spontaneous, adapt-able, and open to new ideas and experiences?

The resulting four traits are arranged into sixteen combinations of personality types.[6] For example, if you are an ESTJ—Extrovert, Sensing, Thinking, and Judging—the following is a sampling of professions that would be a good match for you.

Military	Business administrator
Manager	Police/detective
Judge	Financial officer
Teacher	Sales representative
Government worker	Insurance agent
Underwriter	Nursing administrator
Trade and technical teacher	

You will excel and become the absolute best version of yourself when you take a strength-based approach to life. Understanding your natural personality traits and making full use of that information is only part of the equation. Next, you should identify your natural talents and abilities.

To better understand your talents and maximize your potential, I recommend CliftonStrengths 34.[7] This resource helps you map out your complete and unique talent DNA, providing interactive learning opportunities. It also provides a common language you can adopt for speaking

6   See all sixteen combinations of personality types and the associated sampling of professions at https://www.iccb.org/iccb/wp-content/pdfs/adulted/tdl_bridge_curriculum/tdl_career_awareness/tdl_career_aware_resource_file/Suggested_Careers_for_MBTI.pdf

7   https://store.gallup.com/p/en-us/10003/cliftonstrengths-34

about your strengths and weaknesses that are good for job interviews and career development discussions with mentors and/or employers.

In order to view a sample report of CliftonStrengths 34 results, go to

https://www.gallup.com/cliftonstrengths/en/253676/how-cliftonstrengths-works.aspx

and click "View Sample" toward the bottom of the page.

MATCHING STRENGTHS AND INTERESTS TO CAREER

Each of us has academic strengths, hobbies, and passions. Let's call these strengths and interests the "Big Three." Maybe your Big Three are talents or strengths you were born with that could be leveraged into an ideal career. In a perfect world, we would all choose a career that makes use of each of our strengths and interests. Too good to be true?

Let's take a look at some examples.

Example 1

Academic strengths – math and physics

Hobbies – playing the saxophone and music in general

Passion – cars

Career target – Industrial engineer for a car manufacturer designing automobile sound systems

Example 2

> Academic strengths – business and industrial arts
>
> Hobbies – water sports
>
> Passion – fashion
>
> Career Target – Swimwear prototype design/test market

Example 3

> Academic Strengths – biology and chemistry
>
> Hobbies – cooking
>
> Passion – volunteering in children's hospital
>
> Career Target – Research on food allergies impacting children

The above examples were provided by Acceleron Learning, where the career targets were identified by using the following technique:

Looking at the above examples and knowing your Big Three, how easy would it be to identify the perfect career? It would probably not be too easy. But if a third party were to noodle about your Big Three, they might make some useful recommendations. Better yet, if a group of five to ten people were to do the same exercise, superior results are likely. So, consider testing the above exercise with your friends. Each person lists their Big Three—without identifying names—and the group suggests ideal career(s). You may have an "aha!" moment. Go ahead and try it—I'll wait.

A special thanks to Gregg Jackson, Chief Strategy Officer

at Acceleron Learning,[8] for consulting with me on this chapter and the book as a whole.

> *"You've got to find what you love. And that is as true for your work as it is for your lovers. Your work is going to fill a large part of your life, and the only way to be truly satisfied is to do what you believe is great work. And the only way to do great work is to love what you do. If you haven't found it yet, keep looking. Don't settle. ... Your time is limited, so don't waste it living someone else's life. Don't let the noise of others' opinions drown out your own inner voice. ... And most importantly, have the courage to follow your heart and intuition."*

—Steve Jobs, Apple co-founder
(Stanford Commencement Address, 2005)

---

8   https://acceleronlearning.com/

MAPPING YOUR CAREER PATH

I F YOU GO THROUGH LIFE without direction, you are aimless. And when you reach your destination, you don't want to have doubts about the journey and choices made or—more likely—choices *not* made. How can you possibly arrive at your desired destination without plotting your course?

A helmsman navigates the course with a rudder. Individuals navigate their course with a life plan. Without a rudder, the helmsman has no control over direction, and without a plan, you have no control over your life's direction. Of course, as time passes, circumstances and the wind change, course corrections will be needed.

Some people have laser-guided focus on their career choice early on, but many do not. If you go to college, by the start of your third year, you should have a pretty good vision about how you will deploy your education in the career of your choice. The good news is that you don't have to figure it all out on your own. Seek out voices of experience to give you a glimpse of possible future outcomes that you want to pursue or avoid.

Some people meandered into their careers or found their way serendipitously. If they had known then what they know now, would they have made different choices?

Most definitely.

Here are examples of major doubts many people have soon after starting their first real job:

-I should have majored in a discipline that was more marketable (i.e., will allow me to earn more money).

-I thought I would like working with young children.

-This job is tedious and boring.

-I shouldn't have settled for something I can do, and instead, trained for something I want to do. Maybe you are headed in the right general direction, but your focus is slightly off. Accounting, finance, and business might have been the right general direction, but because of the many different flavors, maybe a mid-career course correction is needed. Maybe you prefer cost accounting over nonprofit accounting, banking over insurance, or auditing over posting accounting entries for a restaurant operator. The same can be true in most professions.

I knew an MD who did not like being a family doctor because many of his patients did not truthfully or accurately describe their symptoms. He then studied to become a dermatologist, thinking he would not depend on patients to describe their symptoms and could instead rely on his training to diagnose their particular skin condition. Then he found dermatology boring, so he studied radiology, which he found was to his liking.

Some people have a general idea of what they want to do (i.e., business)—management, accounting, finance, HR, tax—teaching, medical, IT, and so on. But they are not more specific. The more specific your goals, the less time you will waste figuring it out during your finite number of years in the workplace.

How do you select the best career path?

Here are several pointers to help you get started:

1. Take aptitude tests to identify your innate traits and abilities that most directly align with professionals in various careers. The results of aptitude tests will suggest a variety of fields and professions for you to consider. When you see the list, you may say, "That makes sense." Think of your relief when your inner self aligns with the aptitude results!

2. Talk to adults about their careers. This is an excellent opportunity to get an inside peek at a large number of professions. You are probably thinking:

   ○ I couldn't do that!

○ I am too nervous!

○ When and where would I find these adults?

○ Why would they talk to me?

Most adults are looking for ways to engage with young people, wanting to share stories about themselves. You might start by talking to an adult at church or other social gatherings. Start with someone you know, tell them you are trying to decide on your career, and ask if they would mind if you ask them a few questions. Here are a few example questions:

○ What do you do?

○ What do you like/not like about your job?

○ Do you think I might like _____?

○ What courses should I take to prepare for a career in _____?

○ Do you get to travel much? By yourself or with a team?

Once you break the ice, the conversation will flow easily, and they may introduce you to other interesting adults.

Attend career fairs. College or high school meet-and-greets are great opportunities to speak with professors and alumni. Check with your guidance counselor at school about additional resources and venues, and watch the local classified ads for job fair announcements.

When you do get that first job offer, remember to consider the entire offer. Money is just one component. Health care, hours, 401k, and things of that nature all need to be factored in. Comparing job offers depends on the individual. For some, a regular forty-hour workweek might be highly desirable, while others go for the money and don't mind working more hours. One size does not fit all.

After landing your first job, you may bounce around for a few years before finding your ideal work home. You can minimize this searching period by understanding and purposefully using that information to stay on course in your career path. All work environments have different cultures and expectations, and you need to find the work culture that fits your personality best.

-Government work is policy and procedural-based, is known to be stable and generally offers a lifetime of employment, but some consider government work boring.

-Start-ups—young companies founded by one or more entrepreneurs—tend to be shoestring operations, meaning they are often not adequately financed, and the concept has not been tested, which often results in failure. You will experience a lot of different activities and responsibilities that can be useful elsewhere, but start-ups are not known to offer long-term, stable employment.

-Turnarounds—companies who recover from loss and become profitable—are intense and risky. You will be exposed to a lot of different activities and responsibilities, but the company has already demonstrated that long-term, stable employment may not be a reality.

-Small companies,—meaning with fifty or fewer employees[9]—will provide exposure to many activities and responsibilities, along with a broader awareness of how the company operates and profits. Growth opportunities are limited by the size of the organization, but you have the potential to be a big fish in a small pond.

-Medium—mid-sized—companies, meaning with between 50 and 250 employees, represent an averaging of the comments of small and large companies.

-Large companies are those in manufacturing industries that employ five hundred or more individuals or those that do not manufacture goods but have an average of $7 million in annual receipts. You will most likely only see a small part of the organization's activities. There are many different ladders to climb, which creates opportunities for lateral moves on your way to the top, and lateral moves broaden your experience and make you more valuable to the organization. You might be a small fish in a large pond for your entire career, but you have the potential to be a big fish in a big pond. It is also worth noting that big organizations pay more for similar titles than small or medium

9   http://www.oecd.org/

companies and have excellent reputations for training employees in the latest IT systems and management techniques.

After gaining experience in a large organization, some people take their experience and move to small or medium organizations where their training is highly appreciated, but after moving from a large to a small or medium organization, it will be very difficult to move back to a large organization. Large companies have infinitely more complex processes than small and medium organizations, and they tend to promote from within to leverage the training and development they endlessly provide. Once you leave that environment, the large company moves forward without you, continuously improving their technology, efficiency and quality, such that you would no longer be "experienced" enough to pick up where you left off if you wanted to return.

Many new hires fail to correctly figure out a company's culture, only to end up leaving relatively soon. Key indicators to research:

- Ask your recruiter why previous employees were successful.

- Ask your recruiter why other people left the company.

- While in the company's offices, notice whether employees smile at you or avoid eye contact. Pay attention to your sixth sense.

- Request a temporary contract position if you

are unsure about your fit into the company's culture.

- Check out websites where employees leave employer reviews, basically explaining their experience while working for a company. Fairygodboss and Glassdoor are two good sites for this type of research.

Is it important to live in a big house with expensive luxury cars and a boat? If so, make sure the income potential of your career choice supports that lifestyle.

Earnings can differ greatly among college degrees. Science, technology, engineering, mathematics, and business can pay up to twice the salary of a liberal arts degree. Follow your dreams to the ideal career choice, but ensure you will be comfortable living the lifestyle your career provides.

Life's choices are about tradeoffs and balance. We all want to love our job and be excited about going to work. On the flip side, wouldn't it be terrible if we hated our job and had daily anxiety at the start of each day? Actual results will most likely be somewhere in the middle. Landing a job that you love is not an exact science. Like hand grenades and horseshoes, close may be good enough, and careful planning will certainly get you closer.

> *"'Learning how to think' really means learning how to exercise some control over how and what you think. It means being conscious and aware*

*enough to choose what you pay attention to
and to choose how you construct meaning from
experience. Because if you cannot or will not
exercise this kind of choice in adult life, you will
be totally hosed."*

—David Foster Wallace, writer and
university professor
(Kenyon College commencement speech, 2005)

NAVIGATING CORPORATE AMERICA I

J EFF ST. PIERRE IS YOUNG, aggressive, and successful. Before college, Jeff worked for a hazardous-materials handling company. After college, he moved to several high-level jobs where he worked for young executives with large egos. This environment resulted in a fast-paced and high-pressure environment full of learning opportunities. Jeff leveraged his experience with the hazardous-materials handling company to found TTN Fleet Solutions. Jeff has tremendous confidence, is extremely perceptive, and offers the following thoughts:

Do not argue with angry people, whether customers, bosses or coworkers. Be empathetic without accepting responsibility, and let the angry person get it out of their system without interruption. Get on the same base as the angry person and allow them to be angry.

Angry customer example:

First rule: Let the customer finish venting without interruption. When there is a pause, interject by saying, "I understand your disappointment in the product. I would be upset if I were in your place." Then maybe, "I would like to discuss your situation with my boss as you may not be the only person experiencing this problem." Ask the customer what he/she wants you/your company to do. If you do not have the authority to satisfy his/her wish, you might say, "If you like, I will check with my supervisor to see if we can satisfy your request. Would that be okay? Please give me your contact information, and I will let you know what my boss/supervisor thinks about your request." In many cases, you already know the answer, but this approach gives the customer time to cool off and heads off the possibility of making the situation worse.

If a customer is unhappy with the quality/specifications of the product, don't argue unless you don't mind losing the customer. It could be that the customer requires a higher grade of product. If you satisfy the customer with a better grade per their specific requirements, you may retain the customer. This is very important since the cost of retaining a customer is far less expensive than acquiring a new customer.

Angry boss example:

Your boss might be angry because your staff has not met their sales goals, has exceeded their expense budgets, is late on their project deliverables, etc. You might reply, "I saw the same thing but have not acted yet. I am watching the situation to gather more information before acting. I need to understand the root cause of the issue before acting."

Don't dress like your peers unless you want to *be* like your peers.

Dress to excel and to climb the corporate ladder. Wear clothes that fit into your office environment, but trend toward the next level up. While piercings, tattoos, man buns, and the like are perfectly acceptable statements of personality, there is nothing personal in business, so consider whether these personal expressions are appropriate and will further your professional goals. Does the boss have a man bun? If not, you should not have one. Dress for the job you want, not for the job you have.

Protect your social media.

In today's online culture, most companies check your social media before making an offer of employment. Remember, social media posts have a long life.

Protect your credit history.

Many companies will check your credit history before making an offer of employment, having found there is a correlation between poor credit history and problematic employees. Poor credit history indicates a pattern of irresponsibility that could lead to distracted behavior due to personal finances. In addition, people with poor credit are not generally hired for jobs responsible for cash handling, accounting transactions, or a variety of other job responsibilities. This may not seem fair, but that is the way of the world. Their reasoning: Employees with poor credit history—and possibly problems with their personal finances—may be tempted to steal from the company if the opportunity presents itself. Think of it this way, if the red flag of poor credit history appears, the hiring manager is exposed to criticism if he ignores the red flag and a problem does occur. Why would the hiring manager put himself in that position?

Your life will be much easier and stress free if you understand and work within the system. Fighting the system will wear you out and get you nowhere. Once you make it to the top, feel free to make changes. But you have to get there the same way everyone else does to be in a position to make big enough changes for it to matter.

Negotiating

Maybe you are a buyer for a retail store, you buy close-out merchandise, or you deal in parts within a manufacturing plant. No matter the job, when negotiating to make a purchase, make the first offer.

Conventional wisdom says that he who makes the first offer loses, but here is the argument for making the first offer: If you are prepared to pay $100, and the seller might want five times that number, the seller cannot—in good faith—say that his item is worth five times your first offer. The seller must now counter with a number that is closer to your first offer.

Note this strategy does not apply to salary negotiations. Each deal may call for a different strategy, so consider the best strategy before negotiating.

When negotiating to purchase a product or service, there are three elements of the deal: quality, speed, and cost. You get to choose two of the three.

NAVIGATING CORPORATE AMERICA II

I MET JAMES LOOMSTEIN AT AN SMU seminar, where a young entrepreneur discussed her successful business start-up. James is an adjunct professor at Southern Methodist University Cox School of Business and a sought-after digital marketing speaker. Loomstein has more than fifteen years of experience in strategic planning, digital marketing and consumer insights. He is a managing partner for Rogue Marketing, specializing in digital marketing. James contributed the following topics during the seminar's lunch break.

Good Bosses

If you have a good boss, count your blessings because there are mediocre or worse bosses in the workplace. Good bosses will support you, recognize your contributions to the organization, protect you—if necessary, from budget cuts, nasty politics, etc.—provide constructive criticism, treat you fairly, and motivate you to be the best you can be.

Good leaders are a rare breed, and you should stay connected with them as long as possible. Hopefully, your good boss will take you with them as they grow with the organization.

Job Loss

It is very likely that you will lose your job at some point through no fault of your own. In the '50s through the '80s, employees spent their entire careers at one company like JCPenney, Sears, GE, GM, US Steel, and other large companies. Today, lifetime employment rarely exists. Every company has its day in the sun and then declines, and this cycle seems to be happening faster. Or maybe your company gets a new top executive, and this person wants their own people that they know and trust. To drive home this point, the new CEO brings in a new VP of Marketing and a new department head. Sometimes, the turnover goes pretty deep. There is a tremendous amount of pressure for top executives to perform, and turnover at the top can occur every two to three years if the company's numbers are not good or if your company is bought or merged with another company.[10]

I joined a fast-growing retail company, Tuesday Morning, Inc., in the early 1990s as part of an entire department renewal. This company had promised the old department personnel a bright future with hefty pay raises and increased responsibility. They were all terminated as part of the department renewal. In order to qualify for severance, each person was required to train the new personnel. Not a nice thank you for their loyal service and extra

10   https://www.forbes.com/sites/forbesagencycouncil/people/jamesloomstein/#3850c22ca7f1

effort on nights and weekends. Nevertheless, our new team made the transition and continued to work magic, grow the company, and accomplish the following major initiatives:

- -Implemented two new accounting systems

- -Refinanced the company's debt

- -Took the company private through a leveraged buyout (LBO)

- -Took the company public (IPO) eighteen months later

Each of those initiatives required a tremendous amount of effort on top of our daily duties. Not long after these initiatives were accomplished, a new CEO arrived and wanted an entire department renewal for our group as well as many other departments. Sound familiar? It happens all the time. This renewal gave us a firsthand perspective on what our predecessors had experienced.

Fortunately, we all found better jobs with an increase in salary and the opportunity to share the knowledge and experience we had gained working for Tuesday Morning, Inc. Since the department/company renewal was outside of our control, we all did our best to embrace the uncertain future. Through it all, we had positive attitudes and faith that things would work out in the long run. We all know that change is hard, but it is inevitable. We also know that difficult times present the opportunity to grow stronger.

Stay curious. The world is changing faster than it ever

has. Skillsets and education that worked well for the baby boomers may not serve future generations as well. Maybe by taking a quick look at where we came from, you can determine where we are going.

During the Industrial Revolution—1760 to mid-1840—machines mechanized work in the textile industry to produce thread and fabric. Iron was needed to make these machines. Iron was later used to make metal bridges and the first ships made of riveted iron plates. As a result of the Industrial Revolution, people began moving off farms and into cities.

From 1840 to 1920, technological progress and economic development created by the industrial revolution continued the economic expansion with improvements in transportation—the creation of trains, steamboats, and automobiles.

After the 1920s, the technological revolution continued with the advent of aviation, space exploration, radio, television, film, telephones, and information technology. It was during this time period that a college degree was the ticket to getting ahead. By the mid-1970s, people were chasing graduate degrees and MBAs for an edge to get ahead. After all, everybody had a college degree. Today, a college degree does not provide the security it once did, particularly if you invest in a major that has little marketable demand.

So where do we go from here? Forecasting is difficult, especially if it is about the future. In other words, I don't have the answer. But I do have some tips that might help no matter the future ahead:

- Be a life-long learner.

- Be flexible and open to new ideas.

- Embrace change.

- Stay competitive and marketable in our fast-changing environment.

- Stay on your toes and be ready and prepared to move quickly.

- Keep your eyes and ears open for opportunity.

- Read books, magazines, respected Internet articles, and think.

- Avail yourself of seminars where smart and successful people are making presentations. Also, be sure to network with the attendees. Trade business cards and write a note on the cards you collect to remember how you connected with the individual. You never know when you will need to reach out to other professionals.

- Stay informed about artificial intelligence (AI). AI may be the next game-changer in the continued technological revolution. Is there a career opportunity in AI for you, or is AI coming for your job? If so, better get moving. Don't get caught flat-footed. Be ready.

Will you be creative and adaptive to capitalize on the next big thing? Cornelius Vanderbilt did just that. Cornelius was born in 1794 and started a passenger ferry with one boat in the Hudson River. He grew the ferry business into a large shipping empire and then sold the business, thinking trains would be the next big thing, and they were. In a world of uncertainty, Cornelius was able to see around the corner in order to capitalize on the next big thing. Today, the world is more uncertain and complicated, which means opportunity for the next Cornelius.

Build a large network of friends. One day, you may need to call a friend with a question, and they will be there for you. I never thought I would write a book, but here I am. I had many questions about the process: where to start, how to find a publisher, an editor, a graphic artist, how much does it cost, and so forth. Fortunately, I have several friends who had published books, and they all gave their unique perspective on the process.

Your questions will certainly be different. If you start a business, you might wonder how to raise capital, why you can't get a bank loan, how long a customer should take before remitting payment, what the legal ramifications of X, Y, and Z are, and so on. If you don't start building your network now, you may find yourself with no one to call for that quick but crucial question.

An acquaintance tells a story about his offspring, whose college roommate stiffed her out of the last month of rent in their senior year, and how the dispute over the rent became ugly. The family who was stiffed was a well-known and respected family in the region with deep connections in the business community. This is the type of friend who rarely comes into your life and should be preserved as a lifelong friendship. What an unfortunate ending to a friendship and potential lifelong network contact over a month's rent. Do not understate the power of all your relationships, not just the ones that appear on the surface to be business-related. They are crucial to your career.

The best place to start building your network is while you are in school. Identify those people who appear most likely to succeed and friend them on social media, but more importantly, in person. How you do this will depend on individual circumstances, but picking the right time is important. Additionally, I suggest a one-on-one conversation. Maybe there is a common thread between you and your target network, such as a study group or an extra-curricular activity.

Be a problem solver. In today's world, most of what you need is available on the Internet—just Google it. It is quite different from the baby boomer's world, where school required substantial memorization and instruction on how to do specific tasks without the benefit of a computer. Many baby boomers did not even have the benefit of a calculator and had to use a slide rule! Just imagine what you can learn from people who had to do everything the long, hard way.

This change represents a huge paradigm shift in the methods and time required to do work and solve problems. Today, one or two people solve problems in an afternoon versus the old days, when a team of people solicited information from experts in various fields. In order to stand out from your peers, be a problem solver and do things that make life easier for your boss:

- Avoid presenting a problem without also presenting a solution.

- Innovate and offer ideas to reduce costs or increase sales.

- Be early.

- Work hard and always present a positive attitude.

- Do what it takes to get the job done without complaining.

- Be supportive of your boss.

- Exceed your goals and objectives.

- Minimize mistakes, but at least learn from them.

LEADERS

"Management is about persuading people to do things they do not want to do, while leadership is about inspiring people to do things they never thought they could."

—Steve Jobs[11]

NO MATTER THE ROLE YOU have now or if you will be starting out in an entry-level position, if your goal is working toward a management position or even just being recognized as a leader among your peers and having more responsibilities, it will be important for you to demonstrate the appropriate leadership qualities in everything you do at all times. The people in your company who can give you the opportunities you are seeking will know what to look for, so desirable leadership qualities—or the lack of—will be apparent even before you have leadership responsibilities.

11 Steve Jobs. AZQuotes.com, Wind and Fly LTD, 2020. https://www.azquotes.com/quote/1059342

Leadership has nothing to do with seniority, titles, or position in the hierarchy of a company. It isn't something only provided by members of management, and it isn't something all members of management excel in just because they are in management. You can have positive and negative leaders—and those who aren't leaders at all—in any scenario in life because leadership is simply the ability to influence others. People with the ability to influence either create a path of positivity or negativity that others around them follow instead of forging their own way.[12]

An employee who exhibits negative leadership qualities might have a tendency to complain in a confident manner and strategic way that causes others to see the same negative views, for example. A very important positive leadership quality is being able to influence others to embrace a big change and make the best of it. Which employee would any company prefer to work with and/or promote?

There are countless resources available on the Internet about leadership qualities and how to develop and recognize each of them, and these lists vary from one to the next. Next are a few common, core qualities that are on most of the lists, and they are the most desirable and best place to start.

Respect

Leadership status is granted, but influence and respect are earned. Setting a good example consistently will inspire

12   https://www.inc.com/travis-bradberry/what-makes-a-leader.html

positive outcomes and directly affect whether you earn respect and are able to influence others. To improve your levels of influence and respect:

- Set a good example. (See the "Do's and Don'ts" chapter.)

- Connect with people empathetically and make them feel important. (See the "Excerpts from Dale Carnegie's book *How to Win Friends and Influence People*" chapter.)

- Build a network of long-lasting relationships. (See the chapter on Navigating Corporate America II.)

Effective Communication

Great leaders know when to talk and when to listen, and they are able to clearly explain their vision and many of the specifics to get the job done. Active listening—including eye contact and expressions of sincere interest—ensures the team feels heard. If you do not listen to your team, they will not follow you.

Confidence

References to confidence are scattered throughout this book. If you lack confidence in a leadership role, people will spot that quickly. The more you believe in yourself, the more you'll be able to manage stressful situations. People will instinctively recognize that and will follow the appearance of confidence. This trait is exhibited more in nonverbal clues—body language—than through words. Standing tall and not slouching, making eye contact, and not fidgeting will be the first things people notice.

Honesty

Contrary to the popular belief that many successful business leaders are inherently dishonest, great leaders treat others as they want to be treated because it's the only real way to make strong connections with others. Dishonest, fake, or insincere habits or practices will quickly derail any career path.

Vision

Jack Welch, former chairman and CEO of General Electric, said, "Good business leaders create a vision, articulate the vision, passionately own the vision, and relentlessly drive it to completion."[13]

You may remember Apple introduced the iPod in 2001, iTunes in 2003, and the iPhone in 2007. Then in 2011, the company was close to bankruptcy. When the iPod was introduced, Apple's stock was just over one dollar, then just under two dollars when iTunes was introduced, and just over twelve dollars when the iPhone was introduced. But Apple's innovation was still alive while the company teetered toward bankruptcy as evidenced by the introduction of iPad, Air Pods, OS updates, and a variety of services including the App Store, Apple Music, Apple Pay, iCloud, AppleCare, Apple TV Plus, and other services that took the stock price to $309 by the end of January 2020. Wouldn't it have been nice to know Steve

[13] https://investorplace.com/2020/03/jack-welch-quotes-to-remember-from-the-former-ge-ceo/

Job's vision in early 2000? Or how about Jeff Bezos's vision for Amazon, or Larry Page's vision for Google?

Every great leader needs a vision they can articulate and drive to completion. Even though you may not be the CEO, you need a vision for yourself and your team. Maybe your vision is to dramatically improve productivity with a new approach or new systems, for example. It takes demonstrating this trait consistently, from the bottom up, to earn the right to make larger changes.

Successful leaders also have a growth mindset. They embrace change and take responsibility for their mistakes while making every effort to learn from them. They are decisive, driven, and focused. You will find so many great resources on the Internet that break down lists of leadership qualities and define them, many with workshopping tools to help you develop your own. No matter if you intend to pursue management roles in your career path, or if you want to punch a time clock—with the goal of earning as much as you can each year on a stable schedule with minimal responsibilities—positive leadership qualities will be the key to your success.

"Great leaders are almost always great simplifiers, who can cut through argument, debate and doubt, to offer a solution everybody can understand."

—Colin Powell,
retired US Army four-star general

"Don't just get involved. Fight for your seat at the table. Better yet, fight for a seat at the head of the table."

—President Barack Obama
(Barnard College commencement speech, 2012)

MAKE LEARNING A LIFE-LONG JOURNEY

WHERE YOU WORK IS WHERE you learn. Experience as many jobs as possible before graduation. Exposure to various jobs will provide perspective on:

- Industries and jobs you may or may not like

- Various management styles

- Experience in the world of work itself

Job hopping while in school is good, but it is bad after graduation. Additionally, experience in various jobs may help you identify something very important to your future job happiness—products or services that interest you.

If you have an internship, this experience will add to your starting salary, and that company may offer you a job upon graduation. An internship with a name brand company could add significantly to your starting salary. An internship will also help you develop skills necessary for the working world, broaden your network of contacts, and sharpen your effective communication skills.

Be a life-long learner in your work and personal life. Certifications, additional skill sets, and master's degrees, etc. will add value to your value.

Four timeless principles that Allen Questrom—former CEO of Federated Department Stores, Neiman Marcus, Barneys New York, and J. C. Penney—discussed in his convocation speech[14] at Boston University School of Business are:

> Dare to be your genuine and trustworthy self. Great leaders and inventors are seldom conformists or imitators. They are original with the courage to look at what is and to dare to envision a better way by thinking outside the square.

> Remember, even if you are the boss, it isn't all about you. The greatest leaders are passionate, purpose and action driven, but they don't succeed by themselves. Leaders provide the strategy, but its successful execution requires investors, employees, and customers buying into the strategy. While managers aspire to top leadership jobs, they need to inspire a lot of people to reach that goal. A successful manager must carefully control scarce resources of time, money, and

14 https://youtu.be/-u09kcffcpQ

people, and that is not necessarily dependent on how smart you are. You will make mistakes along the way because no one is perfect. This is part of the learning process, and it's what you do with your mistakes that will matter most in the long run. Admit that you don't have all the answers. The best leaders surround themselves with the best people, so that they know whom to go to when they don't know the answers. No one gets to where they are on their own. The sooner you recognize this, the more effectively you'll demonstrate leadership qualities.

Any business is a people business. Managers can get bogged down in managing and miss opportunities in plain sight, like empowering our employees and customers by seeking them out, walking around with them, asking them a lot of questions about the business or the product, really listening to the answers, being present … and observing their concerns and reactions. This not only gives the manager a lot of … essential information, but also draws everyone into the team effort, making it their game.

Get your head out of your apps. Make time for a personal life that includes a significant other. As much as technology can do for us, it cannot make us lovable, so put down the phone and treat romance as if it were a start-up. Once you have romanced and caught the partner of your dreams, don't assume that the deal is done. Keep romance alive and you will be rewarded. Humanize and personalize yourself. Believe in yourself, lose the fear and find the courage to take risks, and finally, be mindfully present. Get your head out of your apps and notice the color of someone's eyes.

A special thanks to Allen Questrom for providing the above ideas and quotes.

"We know that today, education is still the key to real and lasting freedom—it is still true today. So it is now up to us to cultivate that hunger for education in our own lives and in those around us. And we know that hunger is still out there—we know it."

—Michelle Obama
(Dillard University commencement speech, 2014)

We grow and learn by doing difficult/unfamiliar things. You might remember how difficult it was to jump into a swimming pool the first time when you were a youngster, but after doing this a couple of times, you found it to be fun. Parents often push their children through situations so they can learn that pushing through uncomfortable things will allow them to grow, and they will one day be able to push through on their own. As you enter the workforce, you will be doing some things that are difficult and will need to push through.

ATTITUDE, PERSONALITY, AND CAPACITY TO LEARN

PHIL HILL SPENT THIRTY-SIX YEARS in information technology (IT), mostly in an executive position with Zale Corporation, Lomas Mortgage, Prudential Mortgage and BNSF Railway. Phil has enjoyed mentoring small groups to large groups of eighty-five. Many of Phil's mentoring materials are sourced from Stephen R. Covey's book, "The 7 Habits of Highly Effective People." Phil is a natural leader and motivator who brings out the best in his team, and he offers the following thoughts:

Attitude, personality, and capacity to learn are things everyone is expected to bring with them to a job. These areas of development are not the responsibility of companies to provide as part of on-the-job training. They will either be assets and skills—or baggage that drags one down—and solely the individual's responsibility.

If you have not yet developed a positive attitude, good personality, and capacity to learn, what then? You can still develop these attributes for your next job or the job after that. Life experience and work experience will teach you if you are open-minded, willing to learn, and if you purposely expose yourself to situations where these attributes are required and consequences for poor performance are implemented.

Some insights:

- -"Not my job" speaks to attitude and capacity to learn. People who aspire to be average only do "their share of the work." If you want to be average, just do your share. People who strive to excel will always do more than their share and produce more than their peers.

- -Dependability is one of the most sought-after traits in any employee. Anyone who can't be available when they are needed—or won't show up for the job—bring little or no value to a company regardless of their abilities, and so they are destined to be replaced.

- -Leave drama at home. Where possible, work out differences with your coworkers without involving your boss.

- -Be supportive of your boss. Bosses can and will be demanding with high standards. Attitude regarding workload does not play well. Bosses have staffing constraints and production and quality needs. But if you are unable to complete your assigned work on time, or if you feel that you are working an inordinate amount of time to complete your tasks, it may be time to take action. If the person who performed the tasks prior to you is still around, they might be helpful in reviewing your work and suggesting shortcuts, but if not, schedule time with your supervisor. Before scheduling a meeting with your boss, prepare a list of your weekly or monthly tasks with an approximate time spent on each task. It might be helpful to indicate if the time spent has increased or decreased and why. Your supervisor may suggest a more efficient approach, identify aspects of your tasks that are no longer necessary, suggest that your efficiency should improve over time, offload tasks to another team member, or indicate that there is nothing he can do to reduce your workload for the short term or even long term. In the end, you may or may not like the answer, but you will have an answer, nonetheless.

-Be a team player and a problem solver.

-Be open to discuss, but don't be argumentative. Once a decision is made, give 100% of your support.

-Anticipate questions rather than be awkward or uninspired. This attribute will help prepare you for promotion.

-Adopt an attitude of persistence to get the job

done. Given the choice, employers often prefer persistence over smart.

-Come in early, stay late, and offer to help with projects.

-Be confident in your skills and abilities, but always have a willingness to learn.

When you change jobs, and you will, be forewarned that potential employers will call previous employers to ask about your work history. Attitude, personality, and capacity to learn will most likely be included in the questions as well as dependability. Even a part-time job or entry-level job can affect future job prospects.

"Nothing can stop the man with the right mental attitude from achieving his goal; nothing on earth can help the man with the wrong mental attitude."

—Thomas Jefferson

TRADE UP TO BIGGER PROBLEMS

OPPORTUNITIES ARE SOMETIMES DISGUISED AS problems in all areas of our lives. All work environments have problems hiding in plain sight. As you might guess, the bigger the job responsibilities, the bigger the problems. So, if you want to move up in your organization, trade your smaller problems for bigger ones. Some examples:

- Volunteer for a tough assignment and work endlessly to solve the problem.

- If your boss comes to you with new responsibilities, be ready and appreciative for your boss's faith in your ability and potential. Don't say it is not your job or raise concerns about your ability to learn and perform the new duties.

- If your company has a reduction in staff, volunteer for one or two of the key responsibilities of the departed employee. Your attitude and initiative in seeking out larger problems may help ensure you are not part of the reduction in force.

- Volunteer to train a new employee, perform an out-of-the ordinary-analysis, help open a new company location, or assist with physical inventories. The more you learn and contribute, the more value you bring to the table.

- If you are a leader, volunteer to head up a task force or assemble a team to solve a problem. If you are not a leader, volunteer to be on that team in a support role.

Another way to frame the bigger problem philosophy is to act like an owner of the company. A friend of mine worked for a small company with a disorganized warehouse. She saw the disarray in the warehouse, and because she took pride in her place of work, she took the time to reorganize the clutter. After a short time, she was promoted to warehouse manager and later to successive management positions. She eventually moved on to own her own successful company.

There are smaller things you can do to act like an owner of the company and set an example for others while demonstrating leadership. How many people walking through the office will step over trash in the aisles? It takes a special person to stop and pick it up, and people will notice. You will be noticed if you make coffee when the pot is empty. They will especially take notice if you regularly leave the kitchen cleaner than you found it. In general, if you see something that needs doing, do it! These small things get you noticed so that you stand above the crowd.

Always keep your eyes and ears open for additional responsibilities and let it be known that you have successfully taken on additional responsibilities in the past. Having a history of taking on bigger problems will put you on the fast track for promotion.

Would this approach benefit you in other areas of your life? I think so. Look for opportunities to try it out. You may be pleasantly surprised by the reactions you receive.

HOURLY VS SALARY MENTALITY

HOURLY EMPLOYEES ARE PAID FOR the time they work with no exceptions. If you're in a well-compensated field with lots of overtime, you could make more than if you earned the same amount each pay period on a salaried basis. Hourly employees are also often able to achieve better work-life balance than salaried employees because their work schedules are generally fixed, with overtime typically being an option. Salaried employees often must cancel plans at the end of their workday to get the job done on time.[15]

On the flip side, salaried employees will often have more and/or better benefit options and typically earn an overall higher income than hourly workers, while also enjoying the flexibility of being able to run personal errands during their shift without "clocking out" or using paid time off.[16] The ups and downs of any business will impact hourly employees more than salary employees, as scheduled

15 https://clockify.me/blog/business/salary-vs-hourly-employment/
16 https://www.careerbuilder.com/advice/salary-or-hourly-wages

and overtime hours may be reduced while the salaried employee will receive the same paycheck regardless of the hours they work.

If you are an hourly employee and aspire to be a salaried employee, better check to see if you have an hourly mentality in case you need to make some attitude adjustments.

Hourly mentality generalizations:

- It's only a job.
- Personal responsibilities are more important than career-pathing.
- Do not expect significant advancement or want additional responsibilities.
- Complaining to management about interpersonal issues isn't off-limits.
- Only owe the boss their scheduled shift.
- Work is drudgery, and it's impossible to get ahead.
- Could be fired at any time, for any reason, so they better sit down, shut up, and look busy.

Salaried/Management generalizations:

- View their job as a career.
- Are ambitious and will work more hours as the need arises.
- Want to move up in the organization and/or earn additional responsibilities.

-Carry more responsibility and stress.

-Make more money and have better benefits and job perks than hourly personnel.

Some people have an hourly mentality, while others have a salaried mentality, and there is nothing wrong with either configuration. Both hourly and salaried employees have reasons for their choice, like the hourly employee who may require a more stable schedule for such reasons as child or senior care, night school, and so on. And all companies need a combination of both. This mentality should just ensure that individuals are drawn to the best fit for themselves.

Salaried employees often have an ambitious appetite for advancement in responsibilities and salary. I had a boss who informed me that the average workweek for salaried staff was fifty hours, but there would be times when I would be required to flex up and work more. And he did not disappoint. I had a heavy workload and many special projects. If your career path is meant to take you into management, and you think you are going to get ahead by working forty hours per week, you're wrong!

The point is that you need to recognize there is a difference between the hourly and salaried mentality and decide which is right for you. And your choice may change over time, so being aware of the pros and cons for both options in your field and/or company will come in handy as life changes.

Whether you are an hourly or salaried employee, advancement opportunities come up from time to time, and senior management decides who gets the promotion. If you want to be on the salaried/management track but demonstrate an hourly mentality to your supervisor, you may not be considered. If you are new to the world of work, you may not understand why Jane got the promotion instead of you. If this is so, it's time for some self-examination, then this is one of those issues to discuss with your mentor. If you understand what qualities senior management is looking for, you are in a better position to prepare to be selected for the next open position.

INTEGRITY

DON'T CHEAT, STEAL, LIE, OR do anything you would not want your mother reading or hearing about on the news or Internet. Your integrity is more important than a test grade or a falsified resume, and the consequences of poor integrity are more costly, in the long run, than buying your own office supplies. Being of high moral character and having integrity also means doing the right thing when no one is watching.

When we are children, we first learn to get our way by crying or throwing a temper tantrum. As we grow older, we find that temper tantrums won't bring the desired results. Maybe our next strategy is to sneak a treat after a parent has said no, and then we learn about the consequences of that bad behavior. As we mature from childhood to adolescence to adulthood, most of us develop a moral compass and do the right thing because we want to feel good about ourselves. We develop integrity.

But not everybody takes the high road. Have you ever:

- Stolen anything?

- Cheated on a test?

- Borrowed money, computer, iPad, tools, or books from a friend and not returned them?

- Cheated on your expense report?

- Not returned a library book?

- Frequently forgotten your wallet when going out with friends?

- Underpaid when the restaurant bill was split?

If you answered yes to three or more, you are headed down the wrong path and drifting in the wrong direction. Maybe you have drift disease and are on the path to the dark side. Whether you've strayed or just not thought about this aspect of being the kind of professional that will ensure you achieve your career goals, this chapter will help with self-examination so you can make the necessary changes.

It's not new or uncommon that average Joes and Janes commit various types of theft in the workplace. Surprisingly, there is also a long list of companies defrauded by senior executives who were ultimately responsible for protecting the company's and shareholder's assets. A small sampling of thefts and bad behavior and the resulting punishment follow:

- A falsified resume discovered after hiring resulted in termination and a "not subject to rehire" on the company's records. Future employment verification resulted in a no-hire by future companies.

- A salesclerk used sales receipts that customers left behind to refund merchandise for cash. This clerk was caught and criminally charged with fraud.

- An administrative worker set up bogus companies and submitted invoices to his employer for payment. This former worker is serving a prison sentence.

- Actress Felicity Huffman is a Primetime Emmy Award winner, a Golden Globe Award winner, and winner of three Screen Actors Guild Awards. She has received nominations for an Academy Award and a BAFTA Award. Felicity is also a convicted felon. She was one of fifteen parents who pled guilty on a conspiracy-related fraud charge in the college-admission cheating scheme. She was convicted and sentenced to fourteen days in prison, 250 hours of community service, a $30,000 fine, and one year of supervised release. In addition, she appears to now be estranged from the daughter she was trying to help into college.

- Accountant Sandy Jenkins was sentenced to ten years in federal prison for fleecing Collin Street Bakery of nearly $17 million. Sandy was sixty-six at the time.

-Dubious accounting practices resulted in the bankruptcy of Enron, a US energy commodities and service company. Enron held more than $60 billion in assets and was involved in one of the biggest bankruptcy filings in the history of the United States. Many top executives were charged with fraud, the harshest sentence going to CEO Jeffry Skilling, who received a twenty-four-year sentence and was required to give $42 million to the victims of the Enron fraud.

-A Ponzi scheme orchestrated by Bernie Madoff produced a loss estimated at $64.8 billion. Bernie, former non-executive chairman of the NASDAQ stock market, was sentenced to 265 years in prison.

Of interest, there is no common denominator for the above thefts and frauds. Their lack of integrity simply made it easy for the following reasons to take priority over doing what was right:

-To get the job

-To get into an Ivy League school

-To relieve debt—likely resulting from living beyond one's means

-To have lots of big presents under the Christmas tree

-To pay large medical expenses

-To fund an extravagant lifestyle

- To stroke one's ego—more is better

- To record fraudulent accounting entries at the request of senior management

The most important common denominator is that the above individuals did not have high moral character, and all found a way to rationalize that their behavior was okay. Did they think about their mother or family and friends reading or hearing in the news or Internet about their actions, and the resulting dire consequences for themselves, their family, company employees—who lost both their jobs and their company retirement monies—and stockholders, who lost their investment in the company? Did these thieves have drift disease, where their misdeeds started with minor theft of a candy bar, which gradually increased in size sufficient to bring down a multi-billion-dollar company? Or was their need so great? Or maybe they were locked into future improprieties once they made the first improper accounting entry at the request of senior management

The answer to why these bad guys did what they did could be any of the above and many more, but there is no excuse for lack of integrity. And the judiciary system had no sympathy for their thefts and frauds. If you have integrity and do the right thing when no one is watching, you will never lose sleep over worrying when the authorities will come for you.

Many companies have both a loss prevention department and an internal audit department. These two departments work on a basic premise that:

- Some people never steal.

- Some people always steal.

- The vast majority won't steal if they think
  they're going to get caught.

With this in mind, loss prevention and internal audit departments put policies and procedures in place—internal controls—to ensure that employee and customer theft does not occur. If theft does occur, the procedures will identify the theft for investigation. The message is: Don't think that you won't get caught.

Some companies have a zero tolerance for theft. Early in my career, I witnessed a pharmacist being terminated for stealing a magazine. That seemed a little harsh at the time. I later learned that this pharmacist had been stealing both cash and medications, but the theft of the magazine was the only item that could be proven. Another company that had hundreds of retail shops, many run by young women, posted in the monthly newsletter an animated picture of a young woman behind bars with the following caption: Who will raise your kids while you are in jail?

Effective?

I think so!

DO THE RIGHT THING

I F YOU ARE LEADING A team and make poor ethical or strategic decisions—or focus on money or power versus what is right—you can destroy your group's willingness to follow you.

Examples:

-A large retail company held a much-anticipated annual warehouse sample sale for its employees until one employee complained about the order in which employee groups were allowed to enter the sale. The CEO decided the solution was to discontinue the employee sales. The same company had two Christmas parties each year, one for the kids and one for the adults. The underprivileged upbringing of the company's founder was the genesis of this generous practice. Because one employee complained that it was unfair since employees with kids received benefits those without kids did not, the

CEO canceled the kids' Christmas party. These two decisions were part of a trend where the CEO did not do the right thing, and as a result, this CEO lost the support of the management team, the employees, and the board.

-I heard a story about a business coach hired to improve an executive's management skills. On the first day, the coach heard the executive speak to a group of managers, sharing a story he'd heard on a nature show the previous weekend. A sick elephant was down, and the other elephants gathered around to protect the sick one and put sand on him to protect him from the sun. The second segment was about penguins. One was sick, and the others gathered around and pecked him to death. Then the executive asked, "What are we?" After a moment, he said, "We are tough like penguins!" The business coach said that you could have heard a pin drop as people in the room were mentally updating their resumes. This company is no longer in business.

You pay the price for poor judgment, maybe now or maybe later.

DON'T SAY THE WRONG THING

David Hayden, restaurant consultant, lends the following advice. Many restaurant supervisors and managers are promoted from the hourly restaurant pool due to their experience and hard work. As a result, their management experience has not been tested. Their management skills have to be developed by trial and error with some help from their supervisor. The following are three things that should not be said by managers of any experience level.

"This Is a Dictatorship, Not a Democracy."

No one disputes the validity of this statement. The manager is there to make decisions and run the show. A business should not be a democracy. At the same time, there are more appropriate ways to express it than to state it in such an uncaring way to the staff. Most dictatorships end in revolutions or coups, with the dictator facing a firing squad. If you refuse to give your staff a voice, they will still speak out behind your back. This is devastating for morale and can spread rapidly. Dictators must live in a state of paranoia, as everyone under their rule is looking for a chance to put a knife in their back.

"It's Not My Decision."

This is the converse of the mentality above. Rather than ruling with an iron fist, this sort of manager avoids any responsibility. They are content to blame their boss, the company, etc. to avoid being the one to upset their staff. The most immediate consequence is for the staff to continue complaining about the decision. Whatever hostility was generated by the decision is made worse because now, not even the manager supported it. When a manager denies accountability in this way, it becomes tougher for them to enforce accountability of their staff. While this is generally done to maintain staff, it usually has the opposite effect. Managers who cannot stand up for a decision actually marginalize themselves by sending the message that they are not really in charge.

"Do As I Say, Not As I Do."

This is by far the most damaging of the three. You will notice each of these three statements is slightly patronizing. All are things you would say to a petulant child. This one makes it clear that a double standard exists. Managers who use this method are really sending a clear message to their staff that they think they are superior. The same rules do not apply because they are in charge. This first calls the validity of the rule into question and then forces the staff to respond in kind. If the staff are treated like children, they will respond in childish ways. When a manager consistently engages in activities for which they discipline hourly employees for doing, they are creating an atmosphere that kills morale.

I will never say that it is easy to motivate employees. I will also never underestimate how quickly the mistakes above can kill motivation and breed revolution. So much of a manager's success is based upon the work of their staff. No manager can do everything it takes to run a successful business on his or her own. It takes a team for a business to succeed. A manager's job is to inspire the best performance they can out of their team. When they fail to do so, the results can range from failure to sabotage to a coup. Leading staff through motivation is not easy, but it is vital.

Special thanks to David Hayden, restaurant marketing and training consultant based in Kansas City, MO. Read more at http://www.themanagersoffice.com/author/david-hayden/

TWO HEADS ARE BETTER THAN ONE

TWO DEGREES OF SEPARATION: ANY two strangers are—on average—distanced by precisely 6.6 degrees of separation. You are one degree away from everyone you know, two degrees away from everyone they know, and so on, so that a chain of "a friend of a friend" statements can be made to connect any two people in a maximum of 6.6 steps.

You will not have all the answers, but someone within two degrees of separation will probably be able to help. If you do not have the answers and nobody else does, ask for help. You will have a better outcome in the long run.

Many professional organizations support open forums on the Internet where you can post messages and ask for help on a variety of issues. In addition, you could pose questions either to an individual or team of people at your company or to an individual in your professional network. Examples of issues posed might include:

- The best software or application for "you name it" to improve efficiency.

- Per diem policy. What are the best practices?

- New standards for accounting issues such as revenue recognition.

- Merchandise return policy. Should our policy be strengthened or relaxed?

Don't be afraid to ask for help.

DON'T BURN BRIDGES

I had a buddy who worked for a fast-growing company but became dissatisfied with the management team. He soon left the company to work for a competitor. Six months later, his old company purchased his new company. Fortunately, he had left on good terms, and he kept his job after the acquisition.

On the other side of the coin, an acquaintance was terminated after a long tenure with a company that was going through some tough financial times and downsizing a large part of the workforce. My acquaintance spoke harshly about his company to friends—and anyone who would listen—and also posted harsh words on Facebook. The result was that he was blacklisted in the business community. Not good when you have a family to support. You may recall from the chapter on Navigating Corporate America I that there was a cautionary statement about protecting your social media. Most companies will check your social media before making an offer, so long before you plan to join the permanent workforce, consider the impact that today's social media post may have on tomorrow's job search.

I live in the Dallas-Fort Worth metroplex, which has a population of 6.5 million. Although a big city, it is a small town when you consider individual professional groups. Everyone in the professional groups seems to know each other or someone in the metroplex's companies. And don't forget, your underling may be your boss tomorrow. The take-away is to always be professional and never burn bridges.

DIGITAL MANNERS

Elements of a good email, according to The Emily Post Institute's Daniel Post Senning in an article in the *Wall Street Journal*:

- -Craft a clear subject line. This is an increasingly important digital courtesy in an age of overstuffed inboxes, as the subject line can help people sort, tag, and find the email later.

- -Use proper salutations and closings. This helps to set the tone for communication.

- -Don't include text-speak: Avoid abbreviations and emojis in emails.

- -Minimize the use of exclamation points.

- -Don't write in all capital letters.

The above might seem obvious, but here is an example of the problem. An eighth-grader sends an email to his teacher that reads, "Hey, can you send me that paper?" With no subject line, no signature, and only a portion of the student's name, the teacher is left to piece together the sender and which paper the student is requesting. This situation provided an excellent example for the teacher to use as a teaching moment.[17]

Texting may be second nature to many kids, but composing an email seems like an ancient craft. That's so last century. But email is still the number one form of communication in the workplace and very important for college and career readiness.[19]

With that said, it is still important to consider generational issues when choosing a digital method of communication. Younger counterparts may prefer texting, while colleagues may prefer email. Think about the age of the recipient and their preferred form of communication—email, text, phone, or other—while deciding the best way to get your message across.

In written composition, tone conveys the attitude of a writer toward a subject or an audience. Tone is generally communicated through word choice and the viewpoint a writer takes on a particular subject. Every written piece comprises a central theme or subject matter, and the manner in which a writer approaches this theme or subject is their tone. Examples of literary tone are airy, comic, condescending, funny, heavy, intimate, playful, sad, sinister, serious, solemn, angry, or threatening.

After you compose your email, reread your composition

17 Jargon, Julie. "Mind Those Manners: Kids Need Lessons in Email and Phone Etiquette: When it comes to making calls and composing messages, a lack of social graces isn't something to LOL about." https://www.wsj.com/articles/mind-those-manners-kids-need-lessons-in-email-and-phone-etiquette-11581417001

for spelling errors, punctuation issues, and proper tone. You might ask yourself if—in your judgment—the recipient will read your email with the intended tone.

Never send an angry email, text, or post. A gym buddy told me about an unfortunate anger email issue at his office. Payroll checks over the Thanksgiving holiday were to be issued on the Monday after Thanksgiving rather than the usual Friday. Although the payroll check schedule was publicized, one of the engineers was furious about the timing difference. As a result, this engineer composed a ranting email in all caps and sent it to all employees of the company.

If you are angry, it is okay to write the email, but wait a few hours to see if you still want to hit the send button. This engineer immediately hit the send button, and soon after, he was terminated and escorted from the building. The engineer's personnel records probably indicate "not eligible for rehire." We all write angry emails or texts from time to time, but everyone feels differently after taking time to calm down from the initial reaction. Remember to act instead of react. Vent to your keyboard, then wait to be sure whether you really want to publicize that reaction or revise your approach to take a more appropriate—and more likely to be successful—action.

Your tone is not always easy to gauge in writing because the body language part of face-to-face communication is not present. Word choices and point of view on a matter—combined with aesthetics like properly capitalized and punctuated sentences versus all caps and sloppy writing—will replace those visual clues. Will the recipient read your email with your intended tone? If, after rereading your email and waiting before hitting the send button, you are still uncertain about the tone, listen to your sixth sense and do not send until you are no longer uncertain.

Remember to act instead of react. Vent to your keyboard, then wait to be sure whether you really want to publicize that reaction or revise your approach to take a more appropriate—and more likely to be successful—action.

"HOW TO WIN FRIENDS AND INFLUENCE PEOPLE"

N 1936, DALE CARNEGIE PUBLISHED, "How to Win Friends and Influence People," which has become known as one of the most successful books in American history.[18] He wrote it during a time when people were moving off the farms to live in cities. People going to work in factories meant working relationships with coworkers and clients became increasingly important. Even written so many years ago, it continues to set sales records each year, serving as a cornerstone for the Dale Carnegie company's professional training and development solutions because so much of his rock-solid advice still has relevance to this day.

Some of the key takeaways from Dale's book summarized:

Be genuinely interested in other people and what they have to say.

Why? Because people are most interested in

18 Carnegie, Dale. *How to Win Friends and Influence People.* Simon & Schuster, 1936.

themselves. Express an interest in everyone you meet or come in contact with, not just the people who can promote you, give you a raise, or help you socially. Showing interest in everyone will ultimately benefit you—try it, and you will see. You may benefit by receiving a warm feeling or by the increased respect of a subordinate or peer. Greet people with animation and enthusiasm. When your phone rings, say "hello" in tones that indicate how pleased you are to have the person call.

Another twist on the above comes from Tim Minchin:

"Respect people with less power than you. I don't care if you're the most powerful cat in the room, I will judge you on how you treat the least powerful... So there!"

—Tim Minchin, Comedian, actor, writer
(University of Western Australia commencement speech, 2013)

Smile often, especially when greeting people, and make sure your smile is genuine.

Don't fake it. Mean it! Sometimes you don't feel like smiling, so then what? Force yourself to smile, and that will tend to make you feel happier too. You have to stand up straight and say it with feeling. Everybody in the world is seeking happiness, and there is one sure way to find it.

That is by controlling your thoughts. Happiness doesn't depend on outward conditions—it depends on inner conditions.

When asked in passing how he was, a well-known CFO in Dallas always answered, "Wonderful." You can't say "wonderful" with your head down and shoulders slumped.

Remember that a person's name is, to them, the sweetest and most important sound.

If you are introduced and forget the person's name, ask that the name be repeated. It is better to ask for their name again than to pretend you know it and not use it.

Be a good listener.

Encourage others to talk about themselves and their interests. Don't interrupt. Use the pronoun "I" less.

Talk in terms of the other person's interest.

When meeting with a client, your first priority is to develop a relationship. If the client wants to talk about sailing, his favorite sports team, Sunday's golf game, the grandkids, or whatever, let him. Don't interrupt. And you will find that when you do talk about business, you will have ample time to do so, and more likely, a reciprocation of attention.

Make the other person feel important, and do it sincerely.

In other words, "Do unto others as you would have others do unto you." Everybody wants the approval of those they come in contact with, the recognition of their true worth, and to feel that they are important in their little world. Nobody wants to listen to cheap, insincere flattery instead of sincere appreciation.

If you are wrong, admit it.

If you are wrong and defend your position, your opposition will come on much stronger to prove you wrong. If, on the other hand, you admit to being wrong quickly, openly, and with enthusiasm, your opposition may take a magnanimous attitude of minimizing your mistake to build their own self-esteem and feelings of self-importance.

As an example, if you are stopped for speeding and admit that you were wrong, the police officer may surprise you with a warning instead of a ticket. The benefits of admitting you were wrong apply in the workplace as well as in your personal life.

If you have an angry customer, your willingness to take the blame for quality or other issues may take all of the fight out of your customer.

If we know that we are going to catch hell anyhow, isn't it better to beat the other guy to it and do it ourselves? Isn't it much easier to listen to self-criticism than to bear condemnation from alien lips?

If your temper is aroused and the other guy's temper follows, coming to an agreement is difficult to achieve.

At times like these, both parties should put their "guns" down and lower the volume in order to calmly and rationally discuss differences. Will you be the leader in this situation to call for everybody to put their "guns" down?

In the second chapter, "A Simple Way to Make a Good First Impression," Carnegie shares an advertisement that was published at Christmas by a department store in New York City:

"The Value of a Smile at Christmas"

It costs nothing but creates much.

It enriches those who receive, without impoverishing those who give.

It happens in a flash and the memory of it sometimes lasts forever.

None are so rich that they can get along without it, and none so poor but are richer for its benefits.

It creates happiness in the home, fosters goodwill in a business and is the countersign of friends.

It is rest to the weary, daylight to the discouraged, sun-
shine to the sad, and Nature's best antidote for trouble.

Yes it cannot be bought, begged, borrowed,
or stolen, for it is something that is no earthly
good to anybody till it is given away!

And if, in the last-minute rush of Christmas buying,
some of our salespeople should be too tired to give
you a smile, may we ask that you leave one of yours?

For nobody needs a smile so much as
those who have none left to give!

HAPPINESS, STRESS, AND GOSSIP

YOU ARE IN CHARGE OF your happiness.

You are in charge of your career and its growth.

You are in charge of your choices.

Yes, there are things outside of your control, but you are in control of your attitude and the choices you make that impact your happiness and your career.

Maybe you didn't get the promotion, and Karen got it. It's natural to feel disappointed or upset at first, but focusing on those personal emotions will not change anything. It won't make you feel better. It won't change that some-one else got the promotion you felt you deserved. Most importantly, not only will it *not* prepare you to seize the next opportunity, it actually might get in your way. You can't be disappointed or upset and not show it. It will reflect in your body language, your attitude, and it won't look anything like the can-do attitude your superiors are watching for in candidates for promotion.

Rather than waste time and energy reacting to any disappointment that might arise from management decisions, use that energy to do a self-assessment. Not because you did anything wrong, but to identify what you can improve upon and add to your skillsets that will make you a better choice for promotion next time. What does Karen provide—attitude, performance, leadership, accuracy, drive, great ideas to improve productivity, etc.—that you do not? Maybe the boss doesn't like you or seems uncomfortable around you, or you don't like the boss or feel uncomfortable around them. Is there anything within your control that is causing this unease? Do you stiffen when the boss approaches? Is your body language defensive, or open and receptive? Are you dismissive to the boss's ideas or directions? What about interactions with coworkers? What are your strengths and weaknesses in influencing each person you work with?

Stress

Don't let superiors, coworkers, or subordinates see you stressed out because they may see this as a sign that you cannot handle your responsibilities. Perception is every bit as important as reality.

Gossip

Don't talk behind anyone's back unless the conversation might benefit company operations or profitability. Wherever possible, keep the target person in the loop. Stay out of company politics and gossip.

Pick your battles

Never put yourself in a position where you win the battle but lose the war. Consider the consequences of your actions. You will encounter situations where the cost of winning a battle is too high, or you won't even know the cost of winning. You may have a difference of opinion with your boss on overtime, workload, an appraisal, dress code, your boss's management style, and so forth, and you may win the argument, but your boss will probably label you as a difficult employee. They may give up on you and start watching for the opportunity to replace you. Every time you raise a difficult and/or controversial issue, you have to ask yourself if the juice is worth the squeeze.

You can only control yourself, not your coworkers and not your boss. There is always something you can change to improve how effective you are, which—in turn—affects how others perceive you. Take purposeful control of the choices you make. Continuously invest in developing your ability to influence the behavior of others, achieving the levels of success and happiness you seek.

"Don't Seek Happiness. Happiness is like an orgasm: if you think about it too much, it goes away. Keep busy and aim to make someone else happy, and you might find you get some as a side effect."

—Tim Minchin, comedian, actor, writer
(University of Western Australia commencement speech, 2013)

LIFE DOES NOT UNFOLD AS PLANNED

WHEN ASKED WHAT THEY WANT to be when they grow up, children often come up with a different answer every week, but these aspirations are rarely achieved. That is no big deal for youngsters. They are incredibly flexible and naturally move from one thing to the next, and they are easily distracted. And it's not real career planning at that stage in life.

As adults, we move through life finding that our personal, professional, or financial life does not always unfold as planned, and this is a big deal. There will be many small and large ups and downs in life, and your reaction to these changes will determine the outcome.

When things happen like the loss of a loved one, loss of a job, or not getting that longed-for promotion, you may experience a major transition. Life constantly throws curveballs. Expect them and be flexible and adaptable.

Stay centered, and don't make changes impulsively. Think it through. Act, don't *re*act.

Also, keep in mind that your logical self may understand and accept the curveballs, but your emotional self may not. To be at peace, your logical and emotional selves need to be in agreement. Sometimes this will happen over time, and sometimes you may have trouble adjusting and need a little help reconciling your two selves. Don't hesitate to seek out a professional counselor to help you through and get you on your feet again. This is money well spent.

Some relevant quotes from graduation speeches follow:

> *"They say everything happens for a reason. I don't know if that's true, but I do know everything happens, and it's up to you to maximize the reality of your situation."*

—Ken Jeong, Stand-up comedian,
actor and former physician
(University of North Carolina, Greensboro,
commencement speech, May 2019)

> *"It is impossible to live without failing at something, unless you live so cautiously that you might as well not have lived at all—in which case, you fail by default. ... The knowledge that you have emerged wiser and stronger from setbacks means that you are, ever after, secure in your ability to survive. You will never truly know yourself, or the strength of your relationships, until both have been tested by adversity."*

—Author J. K. Rowling
(Harvard University commencement speech, 2008)

"If you love only yourself, you will serve only yourself. And you will have only yourself. So no more winning. Instead, try to love others and serve others, and hopefully find those who love and serve you in return."

—Stephen Colbert, comedian
(Northwestern University commencement speech, 2011)

"There's a difference between gifts and choices. Cleverness is a gift, kindness is a choice."

—Jeff Bezos, founder, CEO,
and president of Amazon.com, Inc. B
(Princeton commencement speech, 2010)

WHEN CAREER PLANS ARE DERAILED

I N 2020, THE COVID-19 PANDEMIC dominated headlines worldwide. Hopefully, all of that is in our rearview mirror by the time you read this, but over the course of your professional career, there will be ups and downs as a result of big impacts on society in general, as there have been for every generation before yours. This chapter addresses what to do if your career plans are derailed due to a fundamental change in the economy.

In February of 2020, the economy was humming. Unemployment rates were low, employers were competing for employees, and the stock market was at a record high. Then in March, "Stay Home" and "Shelter in Place" federal, state, and county orders became the new normal. Unemployment rates shot up to historic highs while the stock market dropped 30-plus percent.

By the third month, there were two opposing views of the economic outcome:

Gloom and Doom/The Sky is Falling

This view assumed a long period of "Shelter in Place," with brick and mortar businesses unable to reopen. The longer the shutdown, the more economic damage there would be. Assuming governments would try to bail out individuals and companies by printing more money, it was believed this would result in hyperinflation and a zombie economy that could take years to recover from.

Recovery is a matter of months away

In May of 2020, states started allowing businesses to open in phases, prioritizing restaurants and product industries in early phases and the service industry—like salons and bars—in later phases, with everyone still observing "social distancing" and heightened cleaning guidelines. With each phase of their plan, if the openings did not result in a spike in COVID-19 cases and deaths, businesses would be allowed to go to the next phase of opening. Since the recovery rate was very high, around 98 to 99%, this scenario seemed more likely.

In the meantime, there was a tremendous amount of suffering. I read about people of all income categories being food insecure and losing their homes due to foreclosures and "mean" landlords forcing renters out. Of course, most of the suffering was at the lower-income levels, but many people—including upper-income families—live beyond their means, so when upper-income families experienced a job loss, they had a long way to fall due to unsustainable/large mortgages and car, boat, and credit card payments, etc. I also read about college graduates who were relying on the strong economy we had to find a job with non-specific/non-marketable degrees, and they were then stuck wondering how they would support themselves.

You may remember that my mantra is "Timing is everything." There are steps you can take to improve your situation in times like the COVID-19 pandemic of 2020. I graduated in the mid-1970s, when the job market was dismal due to persistent high inflation and stagnant demand in the economy, which is known as stagflation. I found a twelve-month MBA program that helped me move forward and be productive until the job market improved, and it worked. You may not be able to find your dream job during times like that, but you can always find ways to be productive and improve yourself. *Do not* sit in your parent's basement playing video games until the economy improves. Doing so will negatively impact your future prospects as well as your motivation. You must push forward to improve yourself in your vocation of choice—or to assume a temporary vocation change that would position you to earn where the demand may be at that time.

Some food for thought to improve yourself and your marketability:

-If you are a casual user of Excel, study to become a power user who is proficient with Pivot Tables, VLOOKUP, graphs, if/then statements, and all the bells and whistles that go with each.

-If you are a casual user of Word, study to become a power user who is proficient with tables, formatting, pulling data from Excel spreadsheets, mail merge, etc. and all the bells and whistles that go with each.

-If you are interested in engineering or manufacturing, take a CAD (Computer Aided Design) course.

-Take a computer graphic course if you are interested in marketing.

-Take a public speaking course, which will improve your speaking skills for most careers.

-Check out what type of self-study might benefit you online or from Amazon's bookstore.

-Learn or improve your foreign language skills.

-Take an online class or courses toward a degree.

-Apply for technical training. Maybe you always wanted to weld or be an HVAC technician or an electrician.

-Ask potential employers what type of study they recommend you pursue to enhance your skills during the downtime.

By improving yourself while the economy recovers, you will be able to answer a potential employer's question when they ask, what did you do during the lockdown and/or economic recovery period? Hopefully, your answer will impress the interviewer. Telling the interviewer that you played video games in your parent's basement will not.

CONSTRUCTIVE CRITICISM

FROM TIME TO TIME, YOU will receive constructive criticism from supervisors, coworkers, friends, and family. For most people, giving constructive criticism is difficult because they realize you don't want to hear it. It is especially difficult if they know you to be someone who puts up walls and can be defensive. If people with your best interests in mind are seeing things that you can't see and that could make your life happier, easier, and better, wouldn't you want to leave the door open for them to feel comfortable telling you?

My dad often said that one should only give advice or constructive criticism in two situations, when it is life and death or if someone asks for advice. I try to live by this mantra like many people do, but you will have periodic performance reviews required by your company. You may also receive intermittent constructive criticism around daily activities, like about a written document, organization of an electronic spreadsheet, an email you sent, an interaction you had with a coworker, etc. Some constructive criticism will either be superficial and easy to fix, well-intentioned but off the mark, or a direct and hurtful hit. Keep an open mind and think about what was said or written so that you do not become defensive.

I remember talking to the Corporate Customer Service Team at Tuesday Morning, Inc. They fielded calls from customers throughout the country all day, every day. Some of the complaints were serious and required immediate action. But I will never forget being told that every call, no matter how trite, has an element of truth the company needed to address in order to provide better customer service. Essentially, the customer is always right—even when they aren't—because it takes meeting their expectations to sell to them. Whether we're talking about customers buying products or services or employees working in exchange for a paycheck, the core concept is the same. Your boss is your customer. If your boss says that can-do attitude you are proud of isn't quite up to par with their expectations, you have to figure out how to appease your customer. So when someone criticizes you, dig deep. You may find that the criticism is right on and that you will be a better person, worker, spouse, etc. if you make some changes.

Constructive criticism needs to be taken seriously, as corrective action can change your life for the better. Think about it. Conflict facilitates change, and not all conflict is bad, just like not all changes are bad. Ultimately, the moment of conflict must result in a change, or it will continue to be a source of conflict. Constructive criticism feels like conflict, but if you embrace it as a positive that informs you on the needed change—positioning you to improve and grow professionally and/or personally—you will be happier and more successful in the long run.

I still remember constructive criticism received over forty years ago from my college roommate that has made a difference in my life. I was such a nerd. In fact, I don't remember much of the compliments and praise received over my career, but I definitely remember the hard-to-hear constructive criticism that ultimately shaped my success and still does. It is important to embrace constructive criticism rather than to run from it. I know this advice sounds easy, but it will sometimes be hard.

DO'S AND DON'TS

"You only have to do a very few things right in your life so long as you don't do too many things wrong."

—Warren Buffett[19]

-Do send a thank you note after job interviews. This will set you apart from the competition. Be sure to consider the age range of your interviewer and use appropriate digital or written methods accordingly.

-Do research typical interview questions and practice your answers before going to an interview. Being prepared will show in your answers as well as how confident you appear.

-Do have an answer for, "Where do you see yourself in five years?" Employers prefer candidates with vision and the ability to effectively communicate that vision, in addition to wanting

19 Warren Buffett. AZQuotes.com, Wind and Fly LTD, 2020. https://www.azquotes.com/quote/40650

to know their investment in training you won't be quickly lost.

-Don't bad-mouth your former boss. If you bad-mouth your former boss in an interview situation, the interviewer will probably wonder what will happen if you don't like him or her. Stay professional.

-Don't criticize or make fun of your colleagues because it will probably get back to them and damage your influence.[22]

-Do ensure that your computer requires a password if you are away from your workstation, and do protect your passwords. You do not want the office jokester sending inappropriate emails under your name or an outsider accessing company files.

-Don't snoop in coworkers' workstations or computers.

-Don't open anyone else's notepads or files without permission.

-Don't steal your coworker's food.

-Do your best regardless of how menial the task! In the competitive world that we live, strive to be outstanding and enthusiastic about all assignments.[20]

-Do work hard and work smart. People who don't work hard may think the other guy is

20 Carpenter, Ben. *The Bigs: The Secrets Nobody Tells Students and Young Professionals About How to Find a Great Job, Do a Great Job, Be a Leader, Start a Business, Stay Out of Trouble, and Live A Happy Life.* Wiley 2014.

just lucky. Maybe luck plays a part, but hard work is more likely the cause of their luck. The harder you pull, the easier it will come.

-Don't ignore your company's policy on cell phone use, and especially don't check your cell phone during meetings.

-Do take your vacation. If your company has a use-it-or-lose-it policy, don't lose it! Do get a reasonable amount of sleep and exercise regularly. There will be plenty of time to party on the weekends, but your top priority has to be your job.[22]

-Don't drink and drive—a DWI may keep you from getting your next job.

-Do align the organizations you belong to with your college major.

-Do join Toastmasters. This is a great way to improve your speaking skills and confidence in speaking to groups. Lessons learned from Toastmasters will pay dividends throughout your career.

-Do stay positive and stay away from those who complain.

-Do think before you act or speak. Remember to act, never react.

-Don't say, "No problem." Say, "You're welcome," "My pleasure," or "Happy to do it." "Problem" is a negative word, while the other choices more clearly convey a positive attitude.

-Do keep your reporting manager in the loop.

-Do choose your friends wisely and carefully. During your formative years, friends have a huge impact on the future you. Pick friends who appear to share similar future direction. You might be drawn to or intrigued by Goths, gamers, gangs, or you name it. If this is not how you see yourself five to ten years down the road, resist the temptation.

-Don't get into an intimate relationship at work. It almost always leads to disaster. Though it can be hard to abide by, personal friendships and relationships should only exist outside of work.

-Do bring a notepad and pen to meetings and be a couple of minutes early.

-Do communicate bad news to your supervisor quickly. Examples include the following: we have been hacked, some accounting files were accidentally deleted, one of the numbers in the month-end closing report is in error, we cannot submit the payroll file to the processor, and the advertising campaign does not appear to be working.

-Do identify those coworkers moving up in the organization and understand why they have succeeded. Always be on the watch for examples of the success you are seeking and learn from them.

-Do read and continue to learn with a growth

mindset. Learn new skills, take night courses, or obtain your degree while working a full-time job. I have known several people who earned advanced degrees while working their full-time jobs by committing nights and weekends to their quests. They earned the respect of family, friends, and coworkers, and ultimately, they received desired promotions.

-Don't be someone people think of as a "know it all." Be respectful and kind when you help others learn and grow.

-Do embrace change—it is inevitable.

-Do accept responsibility for your failures and make it a point to learn from them.

-Do show gratitude rather than a sense of entitlement.

-Do Google Successful People to obtain insight into their traits.

-Be prepared to work for your paycheck!

-Don't call in sick when you are not sick.

-Don't involve yourself in office gossip.

-Don't discuss confidential matters outside of the inner circle of confidentiality. Discussing merger and acquisition plans, salary data, planned terminations, store closing and so forth outside of the inner circle of confidentiality can get you fired.

-Don't spend your productive years backpacking through Europe or on a sabbatical. When you return from your travels and are ready to enter or reenter the workforce, expect that a prospective employer will ask what you have been doing over the past three to five years. If you have not been motivated to work and move your career forward consistently, without gaps, many employers will see that as a lack of motivation and will not be inclined to hire you.

-Do work hard and work smart. Check and double-check to ensure your work is free of errors. Companies already have a recipe for success by the time you join their team. Follow and/or exceed all steps in the recipe and don't cut corners.

- When at company social events such as Christmas parties, picnics, golf outings, client dinners, off-site meetings, seminars, or conventions, your actions are being watched. Things to avoid:

- Heavy drinking

- Late morning arrivals due to late evenings

- Sleeping during seminars or convention sessions

- Getting drunk on the golf course and driving your golf cart on the green of your boss's country club—this will get you fired!

○ Sleeping around with company personnel. Do you want a career or a good time? It can't be both.

- Do remember mantras that have significance to you. Mine is "Timing is Everything."

THINGS THAT MATTER

Save as much as you can for as long as you can as soon as you can, and always spend less than you have coming in, forever. This alone will keep you financially secure!

Remember: The things that don't matter, don't matter.

Well-known speaker, philosopher, and author George Addair is quoted as saying: "Everything you've ever wanted is on the other side of fear."

> *"Amateurs practice until they can get it right; professionals practice until they can't get it wrong."*

> —Harold Craxton, one-time professor at the Royal Academy of Music
> (Aug 29, 2013)

RECOMMENDED BOOKS

If I Knew Then What I Know Now by Richard Edler

How to Win Friends and Influence People by Dale Carnegie

The Introvert Advantage – How to Thrive in an Extrovert World (If You Are an Introvert) by Marti Olsen Laney, Psy.D.

Seven Habits of Successful People by Steven Covey

OUR BAD. Why Practical Life Skills Are Missing, and What to Do About It by Ryan Jackson

For Men Only by Shaunti and Jeff Feldhahn (short quick read to better understand the opposite sex)

For Women Only by Shaunti Feldhahn (short quick read to better understand the opposite sex)

The One Minute Manager by Keneth Blanchard, Ph.d. and Spencer Johnson, M.D.

The Bigs by Ben Carpenter

ABOUT THE AUTHOR

Alan L Oppenheimer, CPA MBA has worked for both large and medium size companies and experienced a variety of management styles and business situations over his 40+ years of professional tenure. Alan also consulted for several companies in situations like mergers and acquisitions, bankruptcy, bank loans, forecasting, and year-end audit preparation.

ACKNOWLEDGEMENTS

For their advice, counsel, editing, and encouragement:

I owe a tremendous gratitude to my professional editor, Debra L. Hartmann, and her team at The Pro Book Editor for guiding me through a process that was surprisingly long, laborious, and technical. Debra was my coach and mentor.

Gregg Jackson and Bob Weir, who are professional writers and also mentored me and stood with me through the whole process. And a special thanks to Gregg, who has a passion for helping young people with his business that does just that (acceleronlearning.com).

Linda Morrissey and Sally Fallis, another set of eyes that did a wonderful job of editing. Many thanks, and a replenished supply of red pins is in the mail.

But none of this would be possible without all those who

contributed their experiences gained over forty years and to those who filled other support roles. Thank you to the following:

Dave Cary	Collette Morrissey
Tom Dubowski	Ken Myres
Richard Falk	Bill Nichols
Tom Gress	Frank W. Oppenheimer
Greg Greiger	Allen Questrom
David Hayden	Steve Rosenthal
Phil Hill	Carl Sewell
Mark Jarvis	Jeff St. Pierre
Trey Knapp	Daniel G, Whitsell
Chuck Larson	Rhonda Wrentz
James Loomstein